T0193922

The Breaking of the *Bread*

DR. JOHN THOMAS WYLIE

authorHOUSE®

AuthorHouse™
1663 Liberty Drive
Bloomington, IN 47403
www.authorhouse.com
Phone: 1 (800) 839-8640

Published by AuthorHouse 05/06/2019

ISBN: 978-1-7283-1100-5 (sc)
ISBN: 978-1-7283-1099-2 (e)

Print information available on the last page.

Scripture quotations marked KJV are from the Holy Bible, King James Version
(Authorized Version). First published in 1611. Quoted from the KJV Classic
Reference Bible, Copyright © 1983 by The Zondervan Corporation.

Scripture quotations marked NIV are taken from the Holy Bible, New
International Version®. NIV®. Copyright © 1973, 1978, 1984 by International
Bible Society. Used by permission of Zondervan. All rights reserved. [Biblica]

Scripture quotations marked RSV are taken from the Revised Standard Version of
the Bible, copyright © 1946, 1952, 1971 by the Division of Christian Education of
the National Council of the Churches of Christ in the USA. Used by permission.

The Holy Bible (1901) The American Standard Version. Nashville, TN.: Thomas
Nelson (Used By Permission)

The Wycliff Bible Commentary (1962) Nashville, TN.: The Southwestern Company,
The Moody Bible Institute Of Chicago

Contents

Introduction

IMAGINE A SCENARIO WHERE the world had forgotten (or overlooked) Jesus. Imagine a scenario where the importance of His death should blur from Christian comprehension. Imagine a scenario in which His forgiving, presence, and victory disappear from our cognizance. Expectation (hope) would evaporate. Sin would abound. Sacrifice for good would stop. The redemptive network would scatter.

That is the reason Jesus founded a solemn ordinance, saying, "Do this in remembrance of Me." The Holy Communion has turned into the dearest experience on earth for the Christian, for there we sense Jesus Christ's presence, reality, sacrifice, and living Body.

While frequently of the service, techniques for cooperation, and theological comprehension change, by and by, the Holy Communion (Lord's Supper) is an extremely exceptional and Holy, Sacred event for every genuine Christian. All should approach it with devout and prayerful dignity and spiritual preparation.

It has been so from the earliest beginning as Luke records, "And they (the disciples) devoted themselves to...breaking of bread..." (Acts 2:42). "On the first day of the week, when we were gathered to break bread..." (20:7). The Lord's Supper (or The Holy Supper, The Last Supper, The Lord's Supper) holds a central place in our Christian worship. Here we shall view the various spiritual aspects concerning the communion.

Reverend Dr. John Thomas Wylie

In The Breaking of The Bread

"They told….how he was known of
them in breaking of bread."
(Luke 24:35)

IT WAS CLOSE TO midnight following one of the most interesting days the world has ever known. Superb things had occurred that day, thus quickly there was brief period for reflection, thus heavenly that had there been an ideal opportunity to reflect, reflection would just have extended shock.

The day was the day of the resurrection. That morning Jesus Christ had become alive once again. The stone tomb was lease, and the dead Savior walked forward into the world and showed Himself to Mary in the garden enclosure. Peter and John had visited the tomb, and had brought back the news of the unfilled catacomb and of that peculiar day.

The place, I accept, was the upper room, the chamber in which Jesus Christ met once and for all with His companions. There was no place on earth increasingly consecrated. It appears to have been the only home the disciples had. There Jesus washed His disciples' feet. There the Holy Supper (The Holy Communion or Lord's Supper) was established. There the early church assembled in prayer. There Pentecost happened.

There Jesus showed up over and over to His own. Never was there a place increasingly blessed. No church was ever more full of a Divine Presence. But then it was only the upper room. Be that as it may, if at any point there was a haven, it was there. Nine men hold up in the upper room. There is wonder in their countenances. They are talking over the unusual occasions of the day, of Mary's message. Maybe they review the most recent night He was with them, of where He sat, of what He looked like, of the tones of His voice as He addressed them, and afterward of how He fellowshiped and passed the cup. In this way the night wore on.

All of a sudden the door opened. The two missing disciples quickly enter. They were not expected so soon. They had gone to Emmaus that day to go through the night, and here they are back at midnight. Something has occurred. What would it be able to be? Is there some new danger? Does some crisp risk approach? There is a demeanor of smothered energy about these two men as they go into the upper room. Right away every man is on his feet. Specifically they are tuning in with their spirits in their countenances. Their hearts beat quicker as they tune in. They regain some composure. It is all so odd and brilliant and glorious.

The men recount the adventure to Emmaus, of how as they went, one went along with them. He motivated them with faith, and they opened their hearts and disclosed to him all. They let him know of their misfortune, and of their Master's torturous killing. At that point He clarified to them the Scriptures, until their souls burned with excited expectation. When they achieve their goal He made as though He would go on, however they compelled him to stop and sup with them. Presently they are portraying the night dinner. With trouble they control themselves as they talk about it.

"He sat down with us, and taking bread in His grasp, He blessed it, and broke it, and as He did as such we saw Him. Our eyes opened. It was the Master! We saw Him for one great, brilliant moment, and after that He vanquished. Yet, it was sufficiently long for us to be sure. It was Jesus. It was He Who was nailed to the tree, Whom we laid in the tomb. He isn't dead. He is alive. We have walked and conversed with Him, and He was known to us in the fellowship!"

2   Dr. John Thomas Wylie

Such was the story the two men told at the midnight hour in the upper room. How it more likely than not excited that little organization, and filled the followers with rapture as they told how He was known about them in the breaking of the bread! Maybe the story does not excite us as it excited them. We have become accustomed to it. The glamor is no more.

Our hearts don't burn so easily. Be that as it may, the message is our own; the way that the magnificence of the presence of the risen Christ got through the boundaries which separate two worlds, and flashed out in cognizant acknowledgment on the faith of His disciples in the bread is for us and for all who love Jesus.

The Revealing Christ

JESUS UNCOVERS HIMSELF IN the fellowship. That was the message. Consider what it more likely than not intended to those men in the upper room! It ought not mean less to His devotees today as we accumulate in holy recognition to share of the images of His enthusiasm.

As they tuned in, the disciples stated: "The Master isn't endeavoring to escape us. He would not cover Himself. He is looking to show His face, and to meet us. The puzzle of His strength is certainly not an uncommon ordeal for the special few in some outstanding and commended minute, however it is for all, and it is to be had in the unattractive long stretches of basic drudge, for He shows Himself in the fellowship."

It was only a portion of regular bread. Jesus Christ took the poor man's admission and made it the image and mechanism of blessing. He joined the most astounding and rarest of profound gifts to the day by day part of poor people, similarly just as He would state: "My best is for all. In the event that one has close to a portion of bread, he may at present have heavenly nature for a visitor."

It isn't something to put stock in a Savior Who uncovers Himself through bread, through the simple charge of the regular life? Jesus isn't a privileged person. He has a place with the poor world, and partners in sacred long stretches of cooperation through the unassuming and modest things of life. Such a Presence changes all, and makes even need itself a ceremony.

As they heard how He was known in the fellowship, the disciples think about that last night when He took bread and blessed it, and stated: "This is my body which is for you." They start to perceive what the Savior implied, that it was anything but a typical feast however a mandate, and that He was to show Himself to them during the time in the eating (the breaking of the bread).

Hence in a sacred dedication they were to speak with Him. The bread was the law's image of His essence. So with amazing respect in their little gatherings they started to watch the Lord's' dinner as a demonstration of faith. The spiritual Presence of the table at Emmanus was given to them likewise, until during the time Jesus has been making Himself known to His disciples in the fellowship.

Christ uncovers Himself to His companions when we consider Him and have discussion about Him and endeavor to serve Him, when in some demonstration of philanthropy or thoughtfulness we minister to others in His name. In any case, Jesus shows Himself to us in the fellowship. He stated: "This do in remembrance of me." To the ardent soul who respectfully shares of the image of spiritual partnership at the blessed table there is allowed a look into the glory. As at

Emmaus, so dependably. Jesus Christ is close, until you can look over the table and see Him.

This is the precept of a genuine Presence which each Christian may love, not the rough fundamental that wine is changed to blood and bread to the flesh at the state so of a cleric, but that the Savior partners Himself with the supernaturally delegated images of His enthusiasm, and through these images which recount the account of His love, and to the those who share in faith, He makes Himself Known. Provided that this is true, would I be able to stand to disregard the holy table (The Lord's Supper)? Would I be able to detest the fellowship season, and approach it with low and normal musings, or with narrow minded and bodily perspectives?

Those two disciples almost missed the blessing. Give us a chance to be careful in case, Christ walking and talking with us, we should miss seeing Him since we don't sit with Him at the table and have Him fellowship of life.

The Christ Who Makes Himself Known

IT IS THE CRUCIFIED Christ Who is known in the breaking of the bread. This is the message of the law. It discloses to us that Jesus died. Those men saw this at Emmaus. There was the print of the nails and thorns. Jesus Christ is mindful so as to disclose to us this. As frequently as we eat the bread and drink of the cup, we do show forth His death till He come.

Be that as it may, it was the risen Christ. That was the exciting news that the two men brought their companions. It was what influenced them to remember the fatigued miles that pivotal night. They came back to Jerusalem not to say: "Jesus is dead!" but to announce: "He lives!" Some assume it has little effect whether one puts stock in the resurrection or not. Such individuals have never had a genuine mandate.

"Now is Jesus Christ become alive once again." No dead Christ could mix the world as Christ is mixing it today. "Lo, I am with you alway, even unto the end of the world!" A dead Christ couldn't satisfy that promise. "Christ ever liveth to make intercession for us," and His prayers are not dead supplications. He has promised to come back once more. He is in His people, in the world. He is unpreventable, unavoidable. Indeed, Jesus Christ lives!

It is the present Christ Who is known in the breaking of the bread. Jesus isn't far away. He is with us. They Lord's Supper is the statute of the eternal Presence. Jesus isn't in the tomb, nor in the removed paradise with some extraordinary inlet of darkness among Him and His own. He is right here. We may not generally understand His essence. We may not see Him. But, it isn't on the grounds that He Himself is unbelievable and His essence invented, but instead in light of the fact that, similar to Mary, our eyes are poor, rather on the grounds that we, as well, are moderate to accept.

Jesus Christ is with us. Heaven is at our doorstep. Jesus Christ is at the communion table. It is generally so. The most odd thing that amazing night occurred as the two men were recounting their story. Abruptly they wound up aware of another presence in the room.

No door had opened, but Jesus was there. They thought they had deserted Him at Emmaus, but He is with them, among them.

He is showing the print of the nails. He is saying: "Peace be unto you!" So it is dependably, in shadowy, spiritual framework, however in genuine securing presence, Jesus is with us.

The Christ Who held tight the cross is at our communion table. Just over, we can hear the thumping of His heart. His hands are touching toward us. We hear His voice. We see His face. He isn't far off. He is here. This is the message of the Lord's Supper.

During temptation, in long periods of sorrow, in distress and need, Jesus is with us to continue and solace, to save us unto the end, until, having completed, we will see Him eye to eye, face to face and know as we are known.

Goodness, for sufficiently spiritual to split far from the subjugation of sense and feel the spell of an inconspicuous Presence, and catch a look at the face Whose smile is paradise! We would see Jesus. May He show Himself to His companions as we assemble around the communion table. May He talk until the heart burns! May He sit at the table and Himself bless the symbols of consecrated resurrection, until faith vanquishes the obstructions which divide two worlds!

The Holy Supper
(The Lord's Supper)

"As often as ye eat this bread and drink this cup,
ye do show the Lord's death till he come."
(I Corinthians 11:26)

———————————

THE HOLY SUPPER TELLS the story of Christianity in the days of the apostles, and in all days since the apostles, in Christian lands and in all terrains, in its obvious thrashings and in its unchallenged triumphs, regardless of whether viewed as a doctrinal framework or a custom of love or a moral upset or passion for a person or an eagerness for a kingdom.

Anyway Christianity might be respected or estimated or interpreted, its whole story is packed into and indivisibly bound up with the basic memorial recognition (communion recognition) of the Holy Supper (The Lord's Supper).

There can be no uncertainty but Christ implied the Holy Supper to tell the story, so that if a day should come when His followers had nobody to show them, the law of the Holy Supper may show them; so that if a period should come when the Church had no songs, no evangelists, and no formal worship, its people may at present meet and break bread and remember Jesus; so that if there should come a time when the Bible itself was taken from them, they may have in this basic commemoration of His dying love a revelation and a proclamation of reality that saves the world.

A Perpetual Ordinance

THE HOLY SUPPER WAS to be perpetual - "As often as ye eat" - was the Savior's word. Its observance was to be frequent. The practice of the early disciples appears to have been to fellowship (break bread together) at whatever they assembled. Nature, be that as it may, breeds hatred, and before long worship was dulled.

The Holy Supper came to be treated as a typical dinner, and there came about a disgraceful state of things which Paul reproaches in this section. In eating, some were hungry, and some plastered (drunken). Along these lines by experience was built up the wisdom of distinct communion seasons in the Church.

The recurrence with which the Holy Supper is to be observed isn't to be settled by any firm principle. A few Churches observe it each Lord's Day, others at interims of from two out of three months. It is surely favorable position in the method for heightened commitment and deepened worship when the communion table isn't approached too often, time after time.

One who takes a look at a great mountain uplift, or looks over a huge scope of untamed ocean, has his spirit mixed; but the individuals who see it all the time before long stop to see it. The Mount of Transfiguration was an extraordinary spot for a spiritual satisfaction, however it was a poor area for a perpetual living arrangement.

The Lord's Supper (The Holy Supper) isn't to be observed so regularly that we lose our magnificent love and cease to view it as holy ground. All things considered, we are not to overlook that it is to bless us, it must be kept over and over, for this was the Savior's command. We are to keep it frequently

Dr. John Thomas Wylie

in light of the fact that our spirits need the help that comes thusly, and on the grounds that the truths the Holy Supper teaches, and proclaims are truths we can't consider excessively nor learn too well.

Such has been the historical backdrop of the Lord's Supper (Holy Supper) as the hundreds of years have traveled every which way. It has been an image along which faith has gone from age to age. It has been an obligation of relationship between Christians in all times of the Christian Church. It has kept alive the blessed flares on the raised area of the heart's dedication.

Kingdoms have gone back and forth. Extraordinary houses of worship have been raised and have fallen into rot. Groups have risen, thrived, and had their day. Mainlands have been found. Man's thoughts regarding the universe have experienced an extreme change. The very development of the race has changed. Be that as it may, through it all the noblest, gentlest spirits have kept this experience.

Under what broadly varying conditions they have kept it! At times in the sunlit open, in some cases chased like wild mammoths, they have fled for spread in caverns and tombs to eat the bread and drink of the cup. Once in a while in some ravishing service of the Church, when the red wine of the cup was offered reparations for with the existence blood of the celebrant,- still through every one of the years the supper experience has been kept by all classes and kindreds and countries and tongues, for its revelation of emptied imagery is a language all can get it.

As they have accumulated high and low, president and national, warrior and minister, natural refinements have vanished, for all have felt the spell of that Presence which makes us one, "The Lord's Supper.

As we go to the fellowship (communion) table, we push our way into this goodly organization whose nearness floods every one of the tides of time, and the melody of whose dedication must not be out of congruity with that which fills the curves of paradise itself.

As we share and break of the bread and of the cup, we go into the communion (fellowship) of each one of the individuals who in all the earth keep the supper, - of brothers and sisters in different houses of worship! How little our disparities when we sit at the same communion table!

We have fellowship with those in different lands, who have been gathered out of the non-Christian countries, with evangelists and missionaries on the outskirts, and furthermore with that multitudinous organization who have crossed the flood and who have gone from the Church militant to the Church triumphant. We are not divided.

In any case, this isn't the only message the Holy Supper (Lord's Supper) articulates. It talks not only of the individuals who keep the communion experience, but predominantly of Him (Jesus) in Whose sweet memory the feast (the supper) is kept.

The Ordinance Of Christ's Death

THE HOLY SUPPER (LORD'S Supper) proclaims the Savior's death. As we take the bread, it talks about His body injured and wounded for us, it discusses the nails driven through His hands and feet, of the thistles which pierced His temples, of the lance that was pushed into His side, of His incredible exhaustion, and of the body brought down from the cross and affectionately laid in Joseph's tomb.

As we touch the cup of wine to our lips, it addresses us of the gore on the cross, of that ruby tide which rinses the blameworthy soul and makes us white as snow.

The Holy Supper demonstrates the death of Jesus Christ. Jesus would keep always new in the hearts of His people the remembrance of His death. He would not have them lose or overlook the least detail or the smallest episode associated with it. At whatever point the Supper is kept, it is as if the statute images would state: "Come, investigate the face of the dead Christ, and love the wounds of the Redeemer!"

It is His death that saves us. The prospect that He cherished us enough beyond words us improves us. The thought of an adoration so undaunted and divine that it didn't move back at the cross gives us trust. The punishment He paid there on the detestable cross frees us from condemnation. What an atonement is the death of Christ!

Thus we eat the bread and drink the cup, and announce that Christ died. This is what Christ's followers have been doing for two thousand years. They have not been attempting to shroud their Leader's passing, or to hide a reality which to the world would appear a specific indication of annihilation. They have been boasting of it.

As believers have gathered through the passing years, they have been stating to one another and to the world: "He died. Our God died." He is the only God in the records of love Who isn't hesitant to have His believers state it of Him, and the reason He isn't apprehensive is that His death is His people's deathless expectation.

The Ordinance Of His Return

THE HOLY SUPPER SHOWS that Jesus Christ will come back once more. It demonstrates His death till He comes. He died, however, He isn't dead. He is coming. Death did not stop Him. The cross was only a station out and about Jesus Christ voyaged. In this way, so distant from being an annihilation, it was a sublime triumph.

What we are to understand by Jesus Christ's return? The Church has been perplexed to know. The early disciples searched for a fast return, but the hundreds of years have traveled every which way, and still the Church stoops with its power toward the coming Christ and supplicates: "Goodness, Lord, delay not, but come!" It can not allude to His resurrection, for it was His ascension promise.

It must mean more than His coming at death when the shadow door opens and we see Him face to face. He is coming in the life of the world, in its laws and establishments, in its foundations and philanthropies, in the very character of its human advancement, in the kingdom that is coming. Must isn't, nonetheless, mean more than this? For the promise isn't till we go to Him, till we resemble Him, till His life hereafter, but till He come. It is a prophecy of the personal return of Jesus Christ.

Jesus Christ is coming! This is the expectation which supported the early Christians, and made them invulnerable. Jesus Christ not going from them, but coming toward them. They feared nothing. Sacrifice was rapture. Oppression was privilege. Affliction was bliss. They stood everything, and died without wail or tear or lament, with a song which stopped not until their colorless lips lost the power of speech.

Dr. John Thomas Wylie

The Holy Spirit addresses us of this magnificent, sublime hope. It proclaims that Christ died, and proclaims that He is coming back again. Jesus is on His way. He is in the world more than any other time in recent memory. He is Christ with a future. He isn't merely a dead Christ with a wilted wreath on the shut entryway of a stone tomb, but He is a living, rejoicing, conquering, coming Christ with a crown and a kingdom.

Let us rejoice and be confident, as we eat the bread and drink of the cup; for each time we keep the Lord's Supper, faith is strengthened and courage increased. All the magnificent, sublime values of the Gospel are affirmed to us as personal and present assets.

The past is holy and the future secure. We ascend with the morning light in our appearances (our faces), and the coronation song on our lips. Jesus Christ is coming. Glory be! Hallelujah!

The Mystical Friendship

"Ye are my friends, if ye do whatsoever I command you."
(John 15:14)

—————

JESUS TALKS ABOUT THE mystical friendship. He doesn't imply that His friendship is a myth, for no fellowship is less mystical, all the more genuine, increasingly generous. Jesus implies that His fellowship is a mystery, and a mystery not as in it is strange, dark, tremendous, but as in it is revealed. It is a thing we could never have known except if God had informed us concerning it.

It is a mystery in the sense Paul implied when, discussing the Christian's everlasting status, he stated: "Behold, I shew you a mystery, a holy mystery, a holy secret, a divine and eternal reality. We will not all sleep, but we will all be changed." In this sense, Jesus' friendship is a mystery, a sacred mystery, a divine and eternal reality God has uncovered (revealed).

It is a statute of companionship, for it is a friendship celebrated each time faith shares of the hallowed symbols of the Savior's passion. Its adoration gleams in the spiritualist, consecrated light of the Communion, and blazes in lambent devotion around the communion table, until that humble altar becomes more heavenly, more glorious than a sapphire royal throne, and its sweet substance fills the heart with a profound and eternal peace.

For this mysterious friendship is none other than the fellowship between the divine and the human, among God and man, between the Savior of the world and heathens (sinners) forgiven. Would it be able to be that such a fellowship exists? Jesus Christ pronounces that it does. Revelation lifts the cloak, and says: "Behold, I shew you a mystery. Ye are my friends." it is a wonderful friendship.

Jesus Christ For A Friend

IT IS A BLESSED thing for us to have Jesus Christ for a companion, a friend - not a judge, not a far away identity hidden in some great authority, not simply a guide or an instructor, a Redeemer, however a companion, a friend. One great friend saves the day. He changes the world, and makes life tolerable, endurable. I review a visit an achy to visit the family companion once made me. He had a dear companion. They and wind up alienated. "What A Friend We Have In Jesus!"

His heart was broken. His life was dove in misery. He was returning to his home, not on the grounds that he had lost his work or his well-being, but since he had lost his friend. What a benefit to have for your friend the Son of God, the supreme Ruler of the world!

We have such a friend. We might not have numerous other friends. We may have a couple of common friends, however, none so poor and modest and ugly as to be without one friend, and that One the best.

The proof of Christ's friendship is as strong as it tends to be made. "Greater love hath no man than this, that a man lay down his life for his friends." Christ appears to state: "I will proof to you that I am your friend. I will die for you, dear soul." And He did. He laid down His life for us. Would we be able to question Him after this? It is less demanding to question the character of God than the friendship of Jesus.

This is the message of the ordinance. It addresses us of the mysterious friendship. It announces that Jesus is our

Dr. John Thomas Wylie

companion, our friend. Do you need a friend? There is Jesus Christ. Do you need somebody to understand and comfort you? There is Jesus. Give Him a chance to be your companion and friend, your nearest, dearest friend. Tell all to Him. Carry on with your life in the fearlessness of this faith, with your day by day experience sweetened and sanctified by the mystical friendship.

Jesus Christ's Friends

IT IS A HOLY, blessed thing for Jesus Christ to have us for His friends. He promises us. He says: "Ye are my friends." He says: "Greater love hath no man than this, that a man lay down his life for his friends." "Therefore I am your friend." But this isn't all. "In this manner ye are my friends,- not my servants, my subjects, not just my messengers, my followers and ministers, however something better, - my friends."

Have I at any point thought of myself as a friend of Jesus Christ? He is my friend, but am I His? Have others at any point thought of me as Jesus Christ's friend? As they have seen me, have they stated: "There goes a friend of Jesus Christ"? Might anything be able to better ever be said of me? Am I as true with Him as He is to me? Am I prepared to confess His cause as He is to support mine? Am I as ready to lay down my life for Him as He was prepared to lay down His life for me?

He has revealed to us the confirmation, the proof of His fellowship for us. It was His death. He has also disclosed to us the verification of our friendship for Him. We are to do His commandments. Might anything be able to be less difficult? We are simply to do His will, to do the things He told us, to practice His lessons, to follow His example, to follow in His footsteps.

Along these lines do we show that we are His friends. Give me a chance to carry out my responsibility as it comes to me step by step, with faith in Him, and I am His friend. It might be something that never wins a cheer from the people about me, but it satisfies Him, that it fulfills Jesus Christ, my reward is finished.

The ordinance is stating this too. "Ye are Christ's friends if ye do at all He commands you." Let us make life sacrosanct with this determination. It isn't sufficient to offer worship. We should likewise do His will. As we do, the little deeds of life, similar to the thistle on Sinai, wind up blazing shekinahs out of which God speaks.

The Treasures Of
The Mystical Friendship

Since we are companions, Christ brings us into His certainty. He says: "From now on I call you not workers, for the hireling knoweth not what his Lord doeth; however I have called you companions, for everything that I have known about my Father I have made known unto you." He shares the incredible insider facts of the universe with His companions. This must be outright certainty. Jesus Christ gives us His. Will I decay to give Him mine?

Since we are His companions, He advances our lives, and makes us productive. He says: "Ye have not picked me, however I have picked you, and appointed you, that ye ought to go and deliver organic product, and that your natural product ought to stay." As we do His will, life is spared from infertility. It isn't hard to be valuable. It is fundamental just to do the Savior's will. At that point we are helpful.

At that point do we deliver organic product, and our natural product tolerates until the end of time. The products of the mysterious companionship never shrink. Anything accomplished for Christ is eternal.

Because we are His friends, Jesus Christ takes us with into His confidence. Jesus Christ clothes His friends with august and royal power. "Whatsoever" is a major word before the royal position of the Almighty. No envoy was ever given such certifications. No delegate of sovereignty had such endless influence. Jesus Christ's friends need only go to God and ask what they will, and it is done.

These are the promises of which the ordinance is the seal. If the sacred symbols of the Savior's passion had a tongue, this is the thing that they would say. This is the thing that Christ accomplishes for His friends. He brings us into His confidence. Shall we decline to let Him? He makes us fruitful. Shall we impede His thoughtful, gracious desires? He invests us with influence. Will we limit His power?

The mystical friendship is a seraphic friendship. Its light sparkles around the communion table. Its melody is melodic in the heart that yields its reverence and adoration at the altar of remembrance. Jesus Christ meets us in the mystery of communion, and says: "I am your friend." Ye are my friends. If you would make me happy, do the things I command you.

Doing them, you will know that God has told me. You shall bring forth fruit that will abide, and you will have power to influence the will of God so that whatsoever you ask of Him will be done." Oh, to be a friend of Jesus Christ, just a friend of Jesus Christ, a good, genuine, true, dependable, faithful, steady friend of Him Who loved me and gave Himself for me!

Jesus Christ Liveth In Me

"I am crucified with Christ; nevertheless I live; yet
not I, but Christ liveth in me, and the life which I
now live in the flesh I live by the faith of the Son of
God, who loved me and gave himself for me."
(Galatians 2:20)

Crucified With Christ

THIS VERSE IN GALATIANS 2:20 is a great declaration. Here
are the startling proclamations, in every one of which a man
(Paul) connects into the boundless and lays hold of the eternal.

"I am crucified with Christ." What a challenging thing
for a man to state! Christ had been crucified! He climbed
the desolate thistle way to that ridge delegated with a cross.
He had hung in conciliatory misery on the detestable tree.
The nails had been driven through His hands and feet. The
thistles had pierced His temples, and the lance head had torn
open His side. In the midnight of His passion for men, His
anguished soul had cried: "My God, my God, why hast thou
forsaken me?"

What's more, presently Paul is stating: "I was there on
the cross with Jesus Christ. I am crucified with Him. Each
throb of misery He felt I have endured. The nails have been
crashed into my hands and feet. The thistles have penetrated
my temples. Into my side, as well, the lance has entered, and I
have had minutes when I could comprehend that desolate cry
of the spurned Christ. It is my cross just as His. See, I bear
about in my body the marks of the crucified Lord Jesus.

It was a devoted and committed soul attempting to state how he loved his Master, announcing that he was so totally identified with Jesus Christ as to be a partaker of His enthusiasm and His passion, as to be marked with the imprints and injuries of Calvary. "I am crucified with Christ." Can we say it? Has there ever been a solitary minute when we were so lost in the Savior as to almost certainly say: "Christ, Christ, none but Christ!"

"Nevertheless I Live"

BE THAT AS IT may, the cross did not slaughter (kill) Christ. It immortalized Him. His foes thought they were putting a conclusion to His influence. They were just making room for Christ to take the position of authority on His heavenly throne. Be that as it may, for His torturous killing, He would before long have ceased to live. In a short time He would have been forgotten.

Paul is stating: "I thought I was dying when they killed me with Christ, but I observe that what I took to be the entryway of death was the door of life. I have never been so much alive. I have turned out to be deathless. My enemies are frail to hurt me. Death itself is incapacitated. I walk through the valley of death, by and by I live."

The cross can't execute Jesus Christ's friends. It isn't the image of death, but of life. It is the identification of everlasting status. The individuals who die for the great purpose for Christ don't die. They are alive forevermore. Death has not vanquished them. It has just made room to the royal position (the heavenly throne of God).

"Jesus Christ Liveth In Me"

"YET NOT I, YET Christ liveth in me." Paul appears to say: "I am the same man I was before I was executed (crucified) with Christ, yet I am altogether different. I am another man. I live on the grounds that I am the manifestation of Him Who is the wellspring of life. I can never die, since Christ liveth in me."

Think about the existence one should live who has descended from the cross to this wonderful experience, who has made the sublime revelation that Jesus Christ lives in him, who has in his very own background the certain evidence that Jesus Christ is risen! Such a one should live as Jesus Christ lived.

If Christ lives in him, he should think as Christ would think, and endure as Christ would endure, and serve as Christ would serve. His sole concern must be: "What might Jesus Christ have me do?"

Might you want to almost certainly say: "Jesus Christ liveth in me?" You can never say it until you have been to Calvary, until you have been crucified with Christ. Nor can you ever state it except if you are eager to carry on with His life and think His thoughts and share His suffering, unless you are willing to take up your cross and follow Jesus Christ. "Jesus Christ liveth in me." My, how Paul is climbing! His hands are on the position of authority (the heavenly throne) itself. It is so with all inside whom Christ lives.

"I Live By Faith"

"AND THE LIFE WHICH I now live in the flesh I live by faith of the Son of God." This is his clarification of his glorious experience. He appears to say: "You are asking how Christ lives in me. It is quite simple. It is a result of faith. I am as yet carrying on with an earthly life. I am human. I am no angel. I am a long way from being a saint. I am in the flesh.

I am liable to law, and plagued by temptations, and supported about by confinements, and perpetually battling against the enemies of my soul. I am nevertheless a man with every one of the frailties and issues of an ordinary human. Be that as it may, the flesh life that I live, I live by faith in the Son of God, and on the grounds that I have faith in Jesus Christ, He lives in me."

Faith is the way in which we go into the life of God through Jesus Christ. Faith is the mystery of everything that is great. It reaches into the infinite. It touches omnipotence and omniscience and omnipresence. It has contact with the eternal. We are still in the flesh. The voices of the flesh are crying in our blood. However, we don't have faith in the flesh.

We have faith in the Son of God. That statement of faith enough, just to have faith in Him enough to be eager to share His cross with Him. That is "religious philosophy or theology" enough. With such a faith as this, the ordinary turns into the vestibule of divinity.

"By faith I am crucified with Jesus Christ. By faith death is vanquished. By faith Jesus Christ liveth in me. For the life I now live in the flesh, I live by faith in Jesus Christ. As I approach my every day work, as I walk the avenues and meet my colleagues, as I carry on with this flesh life, I live not as an angel, for I am a far from being sanctified, but I do live by faith. I utterly believe in the Son of God that He has become a part of me, that He has become my life, until His very wounds are mine."

"Who Loved Me And Gave Himself For Me"

THE SECRET IS OUT. It is love. That is what is behind faith. As Paul closes the sentence, he gives the secret away. There is a man hanging on a cross, however behind the cross is a man death can't murder, and behind the man death can't murder is Jesus Christ, and behind Jesus Christ is faith, and behind faith is love. Because there is love, it is anything but difficult to have faith, and in light of the fact that there is faith, it is anything but difficult to have Jesus Christ, and in light of the fact that there is Christ, it is anything but difficult to have life, and on the grounds that there is life, the cross isn't vanquish, however "victory." "Who loved me and gave himself for me."

It isn't difficult to have faith in one who does that for you. It is anything but difficult to confide in somebody who considers more you than of his own life. "Greater love hath no man than this, that a man lay down his life for his friends." Paul is saying that as he saw Jesus Christ hanging on the tree, he found that He was dying for him.

Then he said to himself: "I must hang beside Him." And so he had his place next to Christ on the cross, and as he did that, he found that Jesus Christ was dying for him, but living for him.

Jesus Christ is the mystery. Thinking about Him, dwelling with Him, following Him, preaching Him, teaching of Him, loving Him, until you resemble Him,- this is the purpose for communion. The ordinance images are saying: "He loved me and gave himself for me." They unveil the eternal mystery.

Has that mystery discovered found expression in my experience? Does Jesus Christ live in me? As I drive down the boulevards on tomorrow, is it with me: "Christ, Christ, none but Christ!" As I approach my work does Jesus Christ live in me? This is the place God anticipates that the world should discover Jesus Christ today - in the lives of His followers.

When Michael Angelo painted his extraordinary pictures in the Sistine Chapel at Rome, rather than painting them on the walls of the sanctuary he prepared the roof with these superb manifestations of his art. But when the people go there to look at the pictures, they don't look upward, but down. At the doorway every one, as he enters, is given a little mirror, and as he walks about he ponders the superb pictures in the dome as they are reflected in the little mirror which he holds in his hand.

Jesus Christ has gone into the heavens, but the mirror is on earth. "Ye are my witnesses." Oh, that they may see Him in my life!

Assuming this is the case, I should share Calvary with Him. I, as well, must be able to say: "I am crucified with Christ; nevertheless I live; yet not I, but Christ liveth in me, and the life which I now live in the flesh, I live by faith in the Son of God, who loved me, and gave himself for me."

The Glory Of The Cross

"God forbid that I should glory save in the
cross of our Lord Jesus Christ."
(Galatians 6:14)

AFTER MUCH TALK AND delayed contention about things
difficult to comprehend, this is the end Paul comes to. Is it a
same end or conclusion?

Is the apostle reasonable or unconventional in his assurance
to wonder in the cross? Is his announcement sound sense or a
fit of hysterics? Most likely a great share of the people of his day
thought Paul beside himself. In regard to general conclusion
or public opinion, he himself appears to let it out, when he
proclaims: "I have become a fool in glorying."

Then the cross was an identification of disgrace. It was a
stone of staggering and a stone of offense. The world viewed
it especially as we presently respect the hangman's tree. It was
a characteristic of ignominy, an image of the punishment for
the most exceedingly terrible of violations. It was the destiny
society visited on the individuals who were too dangerous to
possibly be kept in jail, and too awful to even think about
being permitted to live.

There is no magnificence in this kind of thing. We would
call the man insane who might flaunt the hangman's tree, who
might take pride in enduring the severest punishment the law
inflicts on a red-handed transgression (sin). In the event that
this is the thing that Paul implies, he is or has more terrible
than hysterics. It isn't what he implies.

He had seen the cross in the light of Calvary, haloed with
the love which redeems the world, blessed by the sufferings not
of a criminal, but of a Savior, Who makes awful individuals

good, rights the wrong, solaces distress, and expels evil from the world. He saw the cross as the image of the sufferings of God for His wayward and meandering children. He heard there the call of the Father for His own.

He observed the cross, not as the image of the punishment society perpetrates on the most exceedingly terrible, however as a token of the sufferings of the holiest and best to save the most exceedingly bad. He considered it to be Jesus Christ had transformed it, into an indication of gallant altruism, and he stated: "I glory in that!" "The cross!"

Is this the brag of an insane man? Is it wild and over the top? Is it eccentric and crazy? Is it the state of mind of a man whose feelings have cleared him from the moorings of sound judgment and standard rational soundness (in other words ordinary sanity)?

Hero Worship

WHAT IS MORE WONDERFUL than genuine heroism and genuine sacrifice? The world reveres heroism. The religion of numerous individuals is still heroism. It would be an agreeable, stale world were heroism and sacrifice to go out of fashion, were the deeds that are brave and unsafe and troublesome never again to be extolled.

I review the intense pilgrims who ever and again hold the focal point of the phase as the world tunes in to their accounts of hardship and valor in journey numerous perilous experiences.

They have opened no new landmass whither the discouraged and abused of earth may escape for shelter. They have made no significant commitment to the arrangement of the great issues of government and trade and social service, nor human or civil rights.

However, the world appreciates them since they have done or appear to have completed a hard thing. They have been sufficiently challenging to risk life in a troublesome undertakings.

This on a divine scale is the interest of the cross of Christ. The cross is the world's best image of heroism. It is the most elevated expression of the life laid down. It is the loftiest standard of unselfish service and sacrifice.

The cross is more than this. It doesn't represent mere spectacular staggering sacrifice, for standard newspaper heroism or to be posted on the web, for infertile endeavor ending with firecrackers and a supper party. Calvary isn't stagy. Its publicity is not intentional but incidental.

Jesus did not die just to be dying. He died to bless people, to make the terrible good, to heal the open sore of the world and exile evil from humankind. There is no such heroism as that of the Man of Galilee, and its possibility down through the ages has been mixing the drowsy beats of a withering world, and lifting men to high goals and honorable deeds. Little marvel that one of the best and best of men should state: "God forbid that I should glory save in the cross of our Lord Jesus Christ!"

What Christianity needs today is a fresh influence of the heroic. It has become delicate and heavy with progress. A modest religion will never save the world. Simplicity and liberality can't address men during the tones of Calvary. The religion the future, similar to the religion of the past, will be hero worship.

The cross represents the heroism of God, Who did not spare Himself in the hardest thing at any point endeavored by God or man. Paul was not glorying in his very own cross. He was not glad for crosses, of unimportant preliminaries, of every day vexations. It was the cross of Jesus Christ that held him. It was the cross on the lonely hill where hung One Who being God moved toward becoming man, Who though rich became poor, Who took the great world up into His heart, Who having lived the sweetest, most attractive life, life, died the saddest and most disgraceful death just to help people, to comfort them and save them from sin and despair.

Paul says: "This is the thing in which I glory, and God forbid that I should glory in anything else!" I think he had his wits about him. We can afford to be energetic over the cross. In the event that there is anything glorious it is the cross. If there is anything worth living for and giving to and dying for, it is the cross.

If there is nothing to which we may declare faithfulness without a blush, and to which we may anchor our eternal hopes without a fear, it is the cross. Glorious cross! "All the light of hallowed story gathers round its head sublime!"

Applause Of The Cross

THE HOLY COMMUNION IS the Church's solemn applause of the cross. In the statute of the Lord's Supper we commend the sacrificial heroism of the world's Redeemer. If we are earnest as we take the bread and wine, it is only a way we have of saying: "God forbid that I should glory save in the cross of our Lord Jesus Christ!"

Save in the heroism and sacrifice of Him Who died to find me, Who gave His life to find my lost soul in the midst of the desolate wilds! Have we made the vow? It is safe to say that we are praying, not for simplicity or achievement, however for a spirit soul great enough to appreciate Calvary?

The communion is a summon to get away from the shop and store and work area and instruments and desk, and study the wondrous cross on which the Savior gave His life. As that cross casts its spell over us, "our most extravagant gains we count but loss, misfortune, and pour disdain on the all of our pride."

Let us understand that glorying, to be authentic, must be more than an expression. For one to say, "I glory," implies unmistakably more than for him to say, "I affirm; I am satisfied; I am glad; I am proud, I boast." It is similarly easy to do that with Calvary. It isn't difficult to stand off and look at it and say fine things regarding it, and state it is wonderful, it is great and glorious.

But that isn't what Paul implied. That is to say, "I am ready to be offered; I long to encounter the cross." Glory is a word for character. When a man says: "God forbid that I should glory save in the cross," he is imploring that the cross may turn into a personal experience.

We are beginning presently to perceive what he implied. He was dead in earnest. He was making an incredible vow that he could pay only with his life. Am I ready to make it, and in a same great manner? God forbid that I should look for a life of simplicity, of childishness, of vain joys, of common notoriety and grandiose show! God forbid that I should draw back at hardship, or dissent at forbearance! There stands the cross. Let me experience it. Let me taste its passions. Let me be influenced by its power. Let me live it and demonstrate its reality.

It isn't easy. It is anything but difficult to sing: "In the cross of Christ I glory," but to experience that melody isn't simple. May God grant me grace to live it! In the holy quiet of a mystic communion with Him Who has made the abhorred cross the radiant symbol of the world's sublimest heroism and holiest sacrifice, may my lips endeavor to make the prayer of the cross! "God forbid that I should glory save in the cross of our Lord Jesus Christ!"

Cross Bearing

"They found a man of Cyrene, Simon by name.
Him they compelled to bear his cross."
(Matthew 27:32)

———————

JESUS CHRIST IS EN route to Calvary. He is going to Calvary to be crucified, to have the nails driven through His hands and feet, to have a monstrous slash torn in His side by a Roman lance (spear) head, to wear a crown of thorns, and to hold tight an unfeeling cross until death comes to bring down the shade on His agony.

He has had a hard night. He had no rest. He came straight from the misery in Gethsemane to His preliminary, which kept going through the rest of the hours of that terrible night, and when day came, it brought just the unpleasant maltreatment of cunning enemies and the scoffs and abuse of an unfeeling horde. Worn, run down, spent, stacked down with the cross on which He is to die.

Jesus stumbles out toward Calvary. He falters and tumbles from sheer weakness. They drag Him to His feet, but He tumbles once more, and again He falls. He can't rise now. His strength is no more. There He lies with the inquisitive group looking on. It was a sight to influence the holy angels of heaven to sob.

Everything occurred at the gate as they were going out. There they met a man who was coming in. He had been out in the country, and he was coming into the city. I like to think he had no turn in that wild night of shame and despise, that his voice was not blended with the calls of the people who yelled: "Crucify Him!" and that his spirit was not stained with innocent blood.

His name was Simon. He was from Cyrene, in Northern Africa. Regardless of whether a guest at the feast or an individual from the Cyrenean province abiding in Jerusalem, we don't have the foggiest idea; but he was coming in as the death watch was going out. What's more, they lift the cross from the fallen Christ, and lay it on the strong shoulders of the man of Cyrene.

Furthermore, presently they are going on toward Calvary. Jesus Christ is on His feet once more, and the man who carries His cross walks next to Him. There they go together, Jesus Christ and His cross-bearer, the Savior Who straightforwardly will be nailed to His death on the cross and from Whose withering lips will sound the loneliest cry that at any point ended the quiet of sadness, and next to Him the man whose strong shoulders have taken from His broken and spent body its weary load and exhausted burden.

I wonder what go between those two as they went out to Calvary. I am not inquisitive to comprehend what the soldiers said, nor am I intrigued by that disgraceful riffraff that hounded His means; however I am keen on the man who carried His cross. Maybe Jesus did not talk. He may have been unreasonably feeble for words. I think there probably was been a minute when their eyes met, and Jesus have His cross-bearera look the beauty and glory of which Simon carried with him to his dying day.

Also, I like to believe that Simon said something to Jesus as they went on together,- only a word to delight the ragged sufferer, to cheer and comfort the tired soul of the worn out Christ.

With this old story before us, I need to make our communion meditation the subject of cross-bearing, for whoever walks with Jesus Christ must carry a cross. That is being a Christian. Some think only of a getaway (escape) and exclusion (exemption). We would be saved not for what we can do, but for what we can get.

We are thinking about the crown, of heavenly rest. In any case, the cross comes first. Jesus Christ made this plain when He stated: "If any man will come after me, let him deny himself, and take up his cross and follow me." In this account of Simon we find what is involved in cross-bearing.

The Horror Of The Cross

THERE WAS THE HORROR of the cross. It isn't there today. The cross has turned into a decoration to be worn by dainty ladies and delicate men. The cross is put into wonderful designs and set with rich gems and make it into a god. The cross highlights music, and decorates engineering, and enhances art. Its horror is no more.

It was not so in the day Simon carried Christ's cross. All the disgrace of the gallows was there. It was the final expression of disfavor or disgrace for the condemned. It represented every one of that was nefarious and appalling. It was the structure in which the extremest punishment was allotted to criminals of the most reduced and most abominable kind. It was impractical for Simon to get away from a sentiment of frightfulness and horror as he found himself marked with the shame of the cross.

As it were, this element of horror withstands for us in the event that we truly comprehend what the cross-bearing for Jesus Christ involves. His cross isn't that image in the recolored glass (stained glass) of the congregation window. It isn't the image that is put at the highest point of the congregation steeple. It is the sacrifice which cuts deeply in the soul.

Now and then it includes the surrender of what is dearest throughout everyday life. As we face our Golgotha and get familiar with the price that must be paid, something of the fright and horror of the cross still stages itself in our experience.

The Unexpectedness Of The Cross

THERE WAS THE UNEXPECTEDNESS of the cross. Simon walked into his Calvary. There was no declaration. It shocked him. He was not in any case an individual from the procession, not in any case a tourist. He was going the other way. There was each motivation behind why he ought to be the last to be picked. In any case, at the same time, he ends up singled out and stacked down with the cross.

Typically it comes as an amazement. The jolt tumbles from the blue. Enduring and torment don't hold on to be reported. They enter without presentation. We never comprehend what tomorrow holds for us. The cross never proclaims its approach. In this, our cross differs from Christ's. His was expected. He ardently set His face to go to Jerusalem. Be that as it may, God benevolently saves us the anticipation. It is sufficient to realize that when the cross comes, strength will be given to bear the load.

The Compulsion Of The Cross

THERE WAS THE COMPULSION of the cross. "Him they compelled to bear his cross." It peruses as though Simon challenged. What had he at any point done to be along these lines trashed? He was taking care of his own business. He is a tranquil, decent citizen. He has nothing to do with the preliminary. They have chosen the wrong man; in the event that they should have a cross-bearer, let him take one of those raspy throated hoodlums who have nagged Him to preliminary and who were so sharp for His conviction. In any case, they declined to tune in to challenge, and Simon is compelled.

There is an compulsion in cross-bearing. You have asked why the load ought to have been laid on you. What have you done to merit it? It doesn't appear to be reasonable. You make your dissent. Be that as it may, it is every one of the a misuse of words. Back to the cross is an incredible mystery. Jesus Christ did not deserve Calvary, but there was no way for Him to get away. Maybe some time or another the shade will lift, and there will be a clarification, however at this point the cross forces. It were less demanding not to mumble. It were better happily to take the cross and follow Him.

The Severity Of The Cross

THERE WAS THE SEVERITY of the cross. Cross-bearing isn't simple. It is hard. The cross is overwhelming. It pulverized Jesus Christ. Simon was worn before he laid his burden down where Jesus was to die and where all burdens slip from tired shoulders, and the exhausted discover rest. However, there is a severity, a hardness, a sternness about crosses. Sacrifice wears a decree face as it brings us to obligation.

But then this is the glory of the cross. This establishes its heroism. Christianity is anything but a shoddy religion. It challenges the best there is in the soul. It calls for hearts that are bold. It doesn't offer straightforwardness and the joys of a delicate life, however it discusses the tempest, the storm, and sternly calls to hardship and trials. In any case, these things which I have referenced are not all. There is another side to cross-bearing.

The Fellowship Of The Cross

THERE WAS THE FELLOWSHIP of the cross. It was Simon's opportunity to walk with Jesus Christ. He left indefinite quality into popularity bearing the cross. In any case, for this, we ought to likely never have known about him. This was first experience with Jesus. What's more, what a cozy fellowship pursued!

This extremely shaft had pushed down into Jesus Christ's tissue currently presses into the flesh of Simon. Some time prior the load was on Christ. It is currently His cross-bearer's. What a bond! Who might contract from such a sweet burden? Welcome the burden that is an obligation of fellowship with Christ!

Who knows but the fellowship of that hour made Simon a Christian? He has achieved home, and is telling his better half the story. He appears to state: "Spouse, I have had an awesome time today. I met a man dissimilar to any I have ever known previously. They were taking Him out to crucify Him.

Furthermore, they made me bear His cross. In any case, He was no criminal. He was the gentlest, most perfect, most wonderful Man I have ever met. He was increasingly similar to God. I have faith in Him." And sooner or later, I extravagant his better half stated: "I have faith in Him, as well."

Thus they took the Hero of Calvary into their souls. They had two children, Alexander and Rufus. The years pass by. They appear to live in Rome now. One day they have a minister in their home.

They learned how to love him, and he considers them his dear companions. What's more, as he closes his letter to the Romans, Paul says: "Salute Rufus, that choice Christian, and his mother, who has also been a mother to me."

Goodness, the fellowship of the cross! This is the manner in which we find Him,- in the fellowship of His sufferings; and as we share our sufferings with Him, we are not depressed or discouraged. We are glorified.

The Memory Of The Cross

THERE WAS THE MEMORY of the cross. Some days Simon forgot. There were many months that were a clear in his life. However, he always remembered the day he carried Jesus Christ's cross. It emerged, brilliant among all an amazing times. It stamped itself always on his memory.

He wanted to consider it, to look for a tranquil spot once in a while and review that great hour when he walked with Christ and bore His cross. The cross lauds memory, and it is memory that transfigures the cross. There is torment at the time, but by one way or another over the long haul, the agony grows dim, and just the wonder remains.

Along these lines the days we value are the days when we suffered with Him. The deeds we prize are the sacrifices we were allowed to make for Him. It is so here. It must be the same in heaven. Thus, one has nothing worth recalling if he has carried no cross for Jesus Christ.

The Triumph Of The Cross

THERE WAS THE TRIUMPH of the cross. Three days had not passed by it showed itself. Jesus is risen. The fire of the sacred evangel starts to spread. By the thousands they are acclaiming the crucified One as Lord and King. As Simon hears about this, he turns out to be progressively pleased with the day he bore Jesus Christ's cross.

This is his distinction in the early church. When they acquainted him with new disciples, this was the thing they said about him: "This is the Simon who carried His cross." It was qualification enough. The cross is progressively triumphant. Our own is certifiably not an acts of futility. The cross isn't our gloom. It is our expectation. It isn't weight, but wings. It isn't punishment, however remunerate. All hail the cross! "They found a man of Cyrene. Him they compelled to hold up under his cross." Are they laying a cross from Christ's shoulders on you? Try not to shrink, dismiss, or turn away. Rather rejoice, celebrate. For if we suffer, we will likewise reign with Him.

Dr. John Thomas Wylie

Peace! Perfect Peace!

"Peace I leave with you, my peace I give unto you;
not as the world giveth, give I unto you. Let not
your heart be troubled, neither let it be afraid."
(John 14:27)

———————————

THIS WAS CHRIST'S LEGACY to His disciples at the communion table. They are assembled in the upper room. Before long they will go to the greenery enclosure. From the patio nursery, Jesus Christ will go to the cross, from Gethsemane to Calvary. There is the incredible shadow drawing closer ever closer, and soon it will cover that little gathering of friends in its sable melancholy.

Jesus has recently initiated the Holy Supper (The Lord's Supper). He is requesting that His friends complete a thing that will shield them from forgetting Him. He wouldn't like to be forgotten, thus He takes the bread and blesses it, and says: "Take, eat, this is my body which is for you; this do in remembrance of me."

After the same manner He takes the cup, and says: "This is the new testament in my blood; every one of you drink of it; for as frequently as you eat this bread and drink this cup, you do show my death until I come."

He would likewise give them something as He leaves them. There at the communion table He makes an endowment. He devises His estate to His companions. What inheritance would he be able to abandon them? What has Jesus to pass on? He has a lot of inconvenience. Will He leave them that? He has a lot of distress, of oppression and privation, of need and misfortune and hardship, of departure and obvious annihilation.

He has this in wealth, and to be sure, His friends will expediently come into ownership of this. In a couple of hours they will escape for their lives, driven here and thither, chased down, in jail, killed. Christ could without much of a stretch have stated: "My trouble I leave you; my trouble I give unto you," and the world could never have endeavored to break His will.

His endowment, be that as it may, was of an altogether different kind. Give us a chance to hear him out as He devises His estate: "Peace I leave with you, my peace I give unto you: not as the world giveth, give I unto you. Let not your heart be troubled, neither let it be afraid." Christ's inheritance to His friends was peace, perfect peace. It was the one thing the world was consistently endeavoring to detract from Him, however the one thing of which He was in fullest and completest belonging when He came to die.

What's more, those men to whom Jesus Christ along these lines conceived His blessed peace never for a minute questioned the truth of the estate. In the years which followed they experienced difficulty, however they likewise had peace. They had privations without end, and risks that were constant, however they were ever garrisoned with the peace of God which passeth all understanding.

What The World Needs

IT IS THE LEGACY we need most. Presence is swarmed with fretfulness and diversion. Life is stuffed with turmoil. There is unrest and disarray on each side. There is difficulty and estrangement. The tempest is on the ocean of life. The waves are irate. Gracious, for rest! For calm! For getaway from contact and stress! For the Master to stand forward as in time long past occasions and state to the irate ocean: "Peace! Be Still!"

Peace is the thing that the world is requiring most in nowadays in which we live. The prayer for peace beats day and night in a tide of unending mediation against the position of authority of God. It groans over the diminishing lips of officers on the front line. It shouts out of the hearts of ladies who have lost their friends and family, and from the stricken essences of youngsters whom the merciless wars have stranded.

It screeches in the shout of blasting shells, and moans in the gloomy thunder of firearms. It begs paradise in an imbecilic sentiment from scarred and demolished fields, from valleys once dazzling, but at this point ruined, from woodland cut somewhere near shot to draining and unattractive stumps. Goodness, for peace! For surcease of hardship! For a conclusion to war and gore! For a touch of the communion endowment of the world's closest Friend in nowadays of the world's most prominent inconveniences!

Also, peace is conceivable. The thing is changeless. Difficulty has just a transitory residency. Inconvenience resembles a cloud that can't last. It resembles a shadow that must pass. Be that as it may, peace is the endless blue in God's sky which mists may diminish, but not destroy.

Peace is the star whose sparkling light all evenings can't extinguish, for peace is down on God's program for our reality, and He Who is to reign for all eternity has stated: "Peace I leave with you!"

The Peace Of Jesus Christ

WHAT IS THE PEACE of Jesus Christ? It is vastly more than getaway and exemption. It is more than having the hurt stifled and the trouble put to rest. Jesus Christ's peace isn't negative, but positive. It is procured not by fleeing from unrest, but by vanquishing it. It's anything but a spoiled harmony. It is the peace of triumph, the peacefulness of a great victory.

It is peace in the midst of the tempest. You have known about a fledgling roost on the pole of a ship that was hurled by wild waves; however the winged creature was not afraid. It is peace like that. You have seen a star sparkle on the edge of a storm, however the star was undisturbed. It is harmony like that. You may have seen the sun sparkle on a scene that was all perplexity and wreck, but the glory of the sunshine was perfect. It is peace like that.

It is the kind of peace Jesus Christ had. Never was there such resistance. The tumult was ever about Him. Be that as it may, He proceeded onward, tranquil, and undisturbed, for He had a peace the world couldn't give nor remove. It is the peace of an inward content, of a spiritual joy, of a soul peacefulness.

The home of joy is in the heart. The heart draws its nourishment from an unseen source. I have seen a tree developing on the exposed cheek of an bare and barren rock on a hill. Through tempest and daylight it stands up undisturbed from its desolate base, lifting verdant branches which cast a liberal shade.

I considered how it lived on such a sterile site, until I found concealed roots which lapped around the rock and fled to rich and smooth soil, and from that shrouded desert spring by mystery lines the tree drew its sustenance. It is so in the life of the soul. Ever and again our parcel is uncovered and infertile, however faith interfaces with shrouded resources, and we are sustained.

The peace of Jesus Christ is the peace which originates from the great reconciliation. We are reconciled to God by the death of His Son. There is no peace until the soul has peace with God. There is no harmony for anything known to mankind until it focuses right. Man's soul centers in his Maker. Along these lines let us have peace with God through our Lord Jesus Christ. Christ builds up peace among us and our eternal Father, and once that peace is our own, all stresses, worries, distractions or diversions lose their power to irritate us.

The Union Of Communion

"This is my commandment, That ye love
one another as I have loved you."
(John 15:12)

_____

THIS IS A SENTENCE from the Savior's communion discourse..
Jesus is giving His disciples His commandment. He isn't
canceling His Father's instructions. He isn't proposing that
His Father spoke amiss when, in the midst of the glimmer and
thunder of Sinai, He roared out upon the race the ten great
moralities on whose enduring strength the future structure of
human society was to be fabricated.

He is stating that notwithstanding these ten words, and
in ideal congruity with them, and surely, because of them, He
has a law to give. It is this: "That ye love one another as I have
loved you."

It is an incredible commandment. Love is the best thing
on the planet, and Jesus Christ's love was the best love on the
planet, and we Christians are to cherish each other as Christ
has loved us. There is nothing higher, holier, diviner than this.

It is the bond which is to bind the dismantled human
race. It is the bond which is to tie us into new unity. It is the
constitution on which is to be sorted out the kingdom of
brotherhood. All these are there. Each conceivable obligation
is pressed into a solitary line. "Love one another as I have
loved you."

Let us do that, and nothing is left undone. Give us a
chance to do everything else, and neglect to do that, and life
remains woefully fragmented, and obligation tumbles down
into vestiges.

In this commandment Jesus Christ fore-gleams a two-folded union. The first is that among Him and His disciples. The second is that between His disciples and one another. There is first the tie which binds us to Jesus Christ, with the goal that Christ and His people are one. At that point there is the tie which binds us to one another, with the goal that Jesus Christ's people are one.

For each situation the tie is love. Christ's people are unified with Him since He has loved out of existence every dividing and isolating boundary. Christ's people are unified with one another in light of the fact that they love one another as Christ loved them.

This is the union of communion. Declaring it, Christ established the Lord's Supper (Holy Supper) to keep it an everlasting ordinance remembrance, so that as often as His followers should meet and eat bread among themselves, as regularly as they should pass the cup, they should symbolize their unity with Him and their unity with each other.

It is this union Jesus Christ would have His people meditate upon and experience as they share of the holy emblems in remembrance of Him.

We Are One With Jesus Christ

WE ARE UNIFIED (ONE) with the Savior. His love for us is such an absorbing and compelling passion that it makes us as much a part of Him as our bodies are a part of us.

We are one with Jesus Christ, so that if He has any legitimacy, it is much our own as His. He has all legitimacy. His is the merit of a perfect righteousness, the righteousness that can never come into judgment. Since we are unified with Christ, Christ's merit is our own.

We are unified with Jesus, so that if He has any standing with God, it is as much our own as His. He has standing with God. He has gone into the "Holy of holies." He is our all-prevailing advocate, so whatever He asks of the Father is done. Our petitions are as prevailing. This is the thing that Jesus Christ implies when He says: "If ye abide in me, and my words abide in you, ye shall ask what ye will, and it shall be done unto you."

We are unified with Jesus Christ, so that if He has any fortune, it is as much our own as His. Everything is His. He is the heir of God, and in light of the fact that we are unified with Him, we are joint-heirs to a legacy incorruptible, spotless, and that will never pass away. All that Jesus Christ has of honor, of dignity and power, of spiritual assets, is as much our own as His; not on the grounds that we have earned it, not on the grounds that we need it; but because He has loved us.

We are unified with Jesus Christ, so if He has any future, it is as much our own as His. All what's to come is in His keeping. He is the King of the destiny of the world. "Of the increase of his government and peace there will be no end." The destiny of His people is likewise.

No big wonder we are informed that "eye hath not seen, nor ear heard, neither have gone into the heart of man, the things which God hath prepared for them that love him."

This is great. Be that as it may, it isn't all. The reverse side of privilege is obligation. Union is two-sided. Not exclusively is Jesus Christ joined to us, however we to Him. Think about what this includes. If we have any standing, any fortune, any future, any influence, any resource of significant worth whatever, it is ever as much His as our own.

We are Christian soldiers of fortune together. We are not our own, for we have been purchased with a price. We have been bought by an extraordinary love. For this we are to praise God in our bodies and in our spirits, which are His.

This is the first kind of union the communion proclaims. For what reason would it be a good idea for us to be hesitant and frightful if this be true? For what reason would it be advisable for us to be frightened as we look out into the immense hurrying universes in the midst of which we appear to be hapless like a bit above water in a sunbeam? We are not lost. We are a part of Jesus Christ, and all is well.

We Are One With One Another

WE ARE UNIFIED WITH each other, so that if any of us has any legitimacy, it is as much his individual Christian's as his own. We are on a dimension as respects our rights. We should not consider ourselves more exceedingly than we should might suspect. Each must regard the other superior to himself.

We are unified with each other, so that if any one has a heap to convey, it is as much his individual Christian's heap as his own. We are to endure each other's burdens, thus satisfy the law of Jesus Christ. One love has made indistinguishable for our entire life interests.

We are unified with another, so that if any one is in risk, in danger or need, either worldly or everlasting (spiritual), it is as much his individual Christian's as his own. We are to pursue Christ along the street set apart by a cross. "As he set out his life for us, so should we set out our lives for the brethren." We are one in our expectations and points, our beliefs and loves, our obligations and commitments.

Isn't this additionally brilliant? We are brethren. We are not adversaries, contenders, outsiders, chance associates, allies. We are more than common companions. "All we be brethren." Our expectations, our feelings of dread, our points are one."

This is the thing that Jesus Christ needs His people to be to one another. Is it accurate to say that he is anticipating excessively? It would be a brilliant thing for us to abide together along these lines, and act toward one another as per such heavenly bonds.

Be that as it may, is it conceivable? We live in a down to earth world. The environment we inhale is soaked with conflict and criticism and doubt and sin. Would it be able to be that such cooperation was ever implied for earth?

It is asking much. The union of communion isn't a customary union. It's anything but a typical tie nor a shoddy cooperation. It is high as God, sacred and holy as Calvary, suffering as time everlasting. In any case, we don't view it as too high with regards to our union with Christ, or too heavenly with regards to claiming His merit and standing before God.

We feel that our union with Christ is conceivable in light of the fact that His love for us is so incredible, so great. In the event that we loved each other as He loves us, it would not be too wild a fantasy to trust that we may understand here on earth this second kind of union. If we are His actual followers, He directions us to love each other after that style,- "as he has loved us."

If Christians would just keep this commandment of love, it would not be important for us to be persistently endeavoring to design some new panacea for the ills of the world. There isn't much space for starlight when there is daylight. Shoddy plans to achieve human fellowship would fall of their own weight if men would just give a little consideration to Jesus Christ's plan.

The union of communion is Jesus Christ's dream for mankind. It is Christianity's gospel for social redemption. It is such a great amount of superior to all others that they can't be thought about. "This is my commandment, That ye love one another as I have loved you." The world is still far, a long ways behind Jesus Christ. Individuals once in a while talk about Christianity being exhausted. They talk about its disappointment. It would be well first to give it a preliminary.

Jesus Christ proposes to light the torch of human advancement with the fire of His own blessed passion, and instruct men to love each other in the equivalent radiant way that He loves all men. Oh, to discover that exercise! It is the old exercise, the extraordinary, high, divine exercise of being brethren. It is pretty much all there is in religion.

As we share of the statute images, as the old story fills our hearts with its favored harmony, let us pray that we may appreciate with all holy people what is the length and broadness, and tallness and profundity, and to know the love for God which passeth knowledge,- that we may love each other as Jesus Christ has loved us!

The New Communion
In The Kingdom

"Until that day when I drink it new with
you in my Father's kingdom."
(Matthew 26:29)

THIS VERSE TAKES US to the communion in the upper room.
Jesus Christ is assembled around the table with His companions
(friends). Over the table falls the shadow of a cross, and into
the hearts of those present comes an obscure dread that soon
their long periods of friendship will be inconsiderately broken.

For three glad years they have gone here and there, up
and down the land together, under the leadership of Jesus,
partaking in the service and glory of a ministry that has
changed trouble to peace. In any case, hostility has hounded
their means, and the night has come for the last act. Before
long they should part.

Here they part, Jesus pledges them to remembrance. He
takes bread and wine and sanctifies them as the images of His
passion, and offers His disciples when they meet, to partake
of them in sacrosanct remembrance of Him. At that point, out
of the blue, they keep the dining experience (the feast). Jesus
keeps it with them.

In future they will keep it, and during the time Christ's
faithful disciples will keep it when Christ Himself is present
only in the remembrance of the hearts that love Him. Be that
as it may, this evening Jesus is there face to face, and hence
they keep the feast.

He is stating: "This isn't the last time I will keep it with
you. The day is coming when we will meet around the table
once more. Until that day when I drink it new with you in

my Father's kingdom." As He said that, the atmosphere of the upper room changed. It became a waiting room to the courts of glory.

The little road outside was never again an obscured back street (blind alley), ending with the disgrace of a malefactor's cross, but an illustrious road twisting to a royal throne. Jesus will die, but He will live. He will push through the grave, and brush past shades, and shake off the catacomb.

He will drink it new with them, with the morning light in their faces, with no shadow across the table, with no dread in their souls, and with nothing to stain or dim the occasion.

He will drink it with them in the kingdom, not in annihilation, however in triumph; not chased by the foe, but serene; not under cover of darkness in an upper room, but on the statures of the free, and in the sunlit open; not with the hirelings of sly priests hunching outside the door to arrest, but with the songs of the invisible choir, and with the serenade of the redeemed; not with a harsh cross there on a skyline of tempest mists, but with the white throne, and light that never blurs, and the peace that never dies.

This was the Savior's promise to His friends there at the communion in the upper room. As they listened, they forgot their hardships. The shoddy room turned into the royal residence of the King. Dread blurred from their souls. Hazard appeared a relic of times gone by. The note changed from minor to major, and the tune from wretchedness to celebration. The transfiguring light of undying triumph fell on their appearances, and the flames of an enthusiasm that was never to be extinguished flared into flame on the altar of their faith.

"Until that day when I drink it new with you in my Father's kingdom." What did Jesus Christ mean by this new communion in the kingdom? Maybe the standard translation is to allude the text to some experience the Christian is to have after death in paradise, and the contemplation is that after this life of torment, and distress, of battle and the contention of fight and long periods of service are over, and no furious floods to clear about us, we shall meet.

Also, Jesus Christ will meet with us, and for the sake of old times we will meet. Similarly as the soldiers today gather around their open air fires, and recount accounts of a war long past, so the veterans of the cross will accumulate with the Captain of their salvation, and with love in their souls, they will keep the feast.

I envision that the substance of this understanding is true, regardless of whether the drapery we paint into it be true or not. Past the stretches of drudge, there is rest. Past the numerous front lines, there is triumph. Past the slopes of battle, there are the statures of peace. After the long march is home.

There in the glory, with triumph on our flags, we shall meet and welcome one another, and our Divine Leader will appear, and "we will see Him up close and personal, and tell the story, saved by grace."

Let us think about this heavenly communion. Is it accurate to say that we are cast down and disheartened, wildly enticed and woefully tempted? Is it true that we are fatigued? Let us dwell on the hour when this will be behind us.

Now we drink the cup in weakness, however, some day we will drink it with fragility all gone; presently in distress, but some time or another with the tears wiped away; now with Satan hounding our steps, but some time day with Satan in chains forever; now with the sound of battle, but some day with cheers of victory, and the faces of home, and the songs of everlasting peace.

But then I wonder, all things considered, if this is absolutely what Jesus implied when He stated: "Until that day when I drink it new with you in my Father's kingdom." If along these lines, obviously the heavenly communion will be one, not so much of remembrance, as of reunion.

Maybe as we think about this communion in heaven, it appears to be shadowy and far away. Is there not an ever closer a more tangible communion that Jesus Christ had as a top priority? I think there is, for Jesus' service concerned itself less with fulfilling dead individuals happy as with making living people God's children.

Jesus came to set up His kingdom in this world, to bring about changes in human society, to lead men to treat each other right. He talks about this again and again. It is a kingdom of righteousness and harmony and joy, whose one law is the largess of love.

It is a kingdom of peace, when war drums throb never again, and battle banners are rolled up, when all men will be brothers, when the Son of Man will never again be a lonely figure, but every life will extend itself along the lines of His character and ministry.

Such a condition of society appears far off, however it is closer than it was, and closer since Jesus Christ has been living in this world for two-thousand years. The kingdom is coming. Governments are changing from dictatorship to republics. War is respecting global mediation. The models of trade are increasingly moral.

Human life is held in higher regard. Womanhood and adolescence are contributed with an additional sacredness. Delinquents are dealt with, not really as hoodlums, but instead as the casualties of horrendous influences for which they are not constantly mindful. For two thousand years we have been praying: "Thy kingdom come," and it is coming.

This is the significance of world missions. It is a way Christianity has of saying that our brothers and sisters in

Africa, China, Russia, Korea and different pieces of the world must partake in the favors of the kingdom.

When the kingdom has come, when society is set up, when humankind are siblings, when brotherhood is never again a dream but a world reality, Jesus Christ says He will "drink the cup new." As we assemble in that clique, as we meet in the perfect brotherhood and fellowship of impeccable fraternity, we will find as we look round the table and look into one another's countenances; that Christ is with us.

There is an old legend that once the Great Spirit visited the Indians whose house was in the foot slopes of a mountain, and that leaving, he promised to visit them once more. Also, that they may remember him on his arrival, he fixed his image in the stone substance of the mountain. It is said that one old Indian idea of the guarantee by day, longed for its night, and looked frequently and restlessly into the essences of his siblings, to see whether he may recognize the highlights of the Great Spirit.

Finally, when the country had been filtered by war, they investigated the essence of this old prophet, and saw there the lineaments of the Great Spirit, who had returned and taken up his residence to the life of his gave adherent.

It is something like this on a better and more fantastic and divine scale which our God has accomplished for us. He visited the race in the Person of the Son of Man, and leaving, left with us the promise of His arrival; and during that time His unwavering devotees have been reasoning of the promise by day, and longing for it by night, and ever and again voicing the petition: "O Lord, tarry not, but come."

Some time or another when the world has been cleansed by harmony, when the kingdom has come, when organization has been set up, men will investigate each other's appearances, and find there the picture of their Lord, Who has returned and taken up residence in the lives of the individuals who are possessed of His Spirit.

This is the new communion in the kingdom. It is toward this that the Gospel moves. This is the great consummation. For this the Christian is living. His thought processes are from a position of great authority. His citizenship is in the kingdom. He is saved by hope, and hope is viewing the vision of the kingdom, and living as if the kingdom were a reality.

In spite of the fact that the Christian eats and dozes in this period of hardship and unrest and struggle, he is living in the kingdom. The intentions of the kingdom drive his life; and sometime in the future, under the spell and administration of the people who have received a vision, the kingdom will be here, and the world will be prepared for the new communion.

What a fellowship that is destined to be, when men will abhor each other no more, When all are one in Jesus Christ! Christ will show Himself among His friends once more, and as He looks around the table, He will say: "Finally I see of the travail of my soul, and am satisfied.

The long holding up is finished. My petition is answered. All that the Father has given me have come to me. Grace has conquered and love has won."

While Jesus Christ will be there, it will at present be a feast of remembrance, for as we think back on the times of contention, on the oust of aged mistakes, on the fallen lifted and the distressing ameliorated and ailment mended, we will see that Jesus Christ has brought it all about. His cross has won the triumph. His love has cast the spell that has changed the world.

Furthermore, as we lift the cup of that new communion in the kingdom to our lips, each heart will love Him, and the song of the feast will in any case still be: "Bring forth the royal diadem, And crown Him Lord of all."

The Necessity Of The Resurrection

"And he began to teach them, that the Son of Man
must suffer many things, and be rejected of the
elders, and of the chief priests, and scribes, and
be killed, and after three days rise again."
(Mark 8:31)

JESUS PROCLAIMED THAT HIS resurrection was a necessity. We
are in the propensity for putting it on a lower plane. Once in a
while we shield it as could be expected under the circumstances,
and attempt to demonstrate that it might have occurred; now
and then as plausible, and we endeavor to demonstrate that it
likely occurred; once in a while as genuine, and we endeavor
to demonstrate its world.

Jesus removes His revival from the conceivable and
plausible, and even out of the genuine domain, into that of
the outright, and says the resurrection was unavoidable.

We are in the propensity for viewing the cross as a need.
We state that it was vital for Jesus Christ to die. But, there are
the individuals who think about the resurrection as blessed; if
true; but who state that whether it be true or not, we have the
cross; thus they brush the resurrection aside as insignificant.
Calvary was the extraordinary reality, Easter morning but the
airy texture of a poet's dream. Such men would do well to sit
longer at the feet of the incomparable Teacher, Who stated:
"The Son of man must rise again."

The cross made the resurrection a need. In the event
that Christ did not rise, His death was thrashing, and our
proclaiming vain. Calvary was not an atonement, however an
execution. In any case, in the event that Christ arose, Christ

died on as a sacrifice, and not as an injured victim, and every soul that trusts in Him is saved.

The resurrection is a need on account of the race. If Jesus Christ rose not, we are of all men the most hopeless. Death is a horrendous void. Be that as it may, if Christ rose, we will rise too. We will meet again the loved "whom we have lost some time." Indeed, we have never lost them. The Savior's words: "I go to prepare a place for you" are not a reverberation from the pulseless residue to ridicule our hopelessness, but hope's harbinger to every broken heart.

Christ's heavenly ministry makes His resurrection a need. He didn't complete His work as the world's Redeemer when He terminated on the cross. He completed His expiatory work, however the service of intercession remains. "He ever liveth to make intercession for us."

But in the event that Christ did not ascend, there is no mediation. Nobody represents us at the royal throne. We don't have anything but our powerless arms and devout dispositions. The bleak adversary we face snickers us to hatred, and makes fate certain. Religion is an inclining mime, and presence a ghastly bad dream.

Jesus Christ's kingdom makes His resurrection a need. Kingdom implies a king. Jesus Christ promised His disciples to return, but in the event that He didn't rise, He will never return. The inclines of Olivet will never excite again at the dash of His blessed feet. The shades of Gethsemane will never again robe Him with respectful quietness as He prays. The eastern sky will never more empurple and change to gold at the greatness of His coming.

His people will sit tight futile for the sound of His voice and the spell of His essence, for He is gone until the end of time.

"I must suffer, I must be rejected, I must be murdered," but in addition: "I must rise again; I must rise to make the cross a crown, to make the tomb afire with light for all who follow Me; to make dying an entryway, and the catacomb a passage into life; to make room to the way of the throne, where I may pray my people into power. I must rise for the kingdom"? Furthermore, He did.

Consequently it is the risen and living Christ we remember in the ordinance which observes His death. If Jesus Christ were not risen, the Holy Supper (Lord's Supper) would plunge us into despairing and depression. Because He is risen, it fills us with the courage of an eternal immortal hope.

The Glorious Death

"Signifying by what death he should glorify God."
(John 21:19)

———————

IT IS POSSIBLE FOR one to glorify God by the manner in which he lives, and except if he does, he isn't probably going to praise God by the manner in which he dies. Death bed repentance is within the scope of probability, no doubt, however there isn't much credit in such a course.

If one's life disgraces or shames God, his death isn't probably going to glorify Him; but if his life be right, it is conceivable not only for one to glorify God by the manner in which he dies, but to make death his supreme and delegated tribute to his Redeemer.

It is something like this that Christ implied when, addressing Peter, He signified by what death He should to glorify God. In general, Peter's life had been to God's glory. Undoubtedly, there were some dim spots. There was the disappointment of his faith when he walked on the water to go to Jesus.

There was the hour when his bragging surpassed his conduct. There was the dark night of heresy and denial. Be that as it may, there had been repentance, and Peter had revitalized and turned into a new man. Be that as it may, Jesus says to him: "Your great chance is yet to come. It will come when you are eye to eye, face to face with death. Then is the hour when you will win your crown."

While Jesus said this regarding a disciple, in a more full and more truer sense He could have said it of Himself. He was just from the cross and the tomb. Recently, He had died. He had held tight Calvary and rested in Joseph's greenery garden, and He returns from it all to state that death isn't mortification and annihilation or defeat, but opportunity and accomplishment, achievement. It is glorious.

The Penal Scar

JESUS CHRIST BORE A penal scar. He was killed with lowness. He endured the disgraceful passing of the cross. In all the historical backdrop of human punishment and torment, it is dicey if there has ever been concocted a method for the death penalty progressively boorish, all the more mortifying to its injured victim, with a greater amount of torment as far as its can tell than death by torturous killing, and Jesus Christ was crucified.

To add to the ignominy of this punitive scar, to extend His disgrace and embarrassment, humiliation and to escalate His annihilation, Jesus was executed between two common criminals. As though to make joke of His sufferings, the warriors who drove the nails into His shuddering fragile living body and push the lance (spear) into the blessed side and pressed the thorn crown on His blessed forehead and watched the spot in case some friend should do something to moderate His torment or calm His pain sat down before the cross on which hung the dying Christ and bet (gamble) for His seamless robe.

In what manner can Jesus Christ ever throw off such an annihilation, a defeat? No doubt the penal scar of Calvary is there to stay, that the disfavor and disgrace which His adversaries put upon Him in His death would either cover His name with blankness, oblivion or stain it with a perpetual infamy. It has done not one or the other.

The Glorious Triumph

JESUS CHRIST'S DEATH WAS His preeminent (supreme) and radiant triumph. it was His sublimest opportunity to glorify God, for Jesus came to die. He instructed and preached, He worked supernatural occurrences (miracles) and shared man's part, but He came to die. The cross was His objective. Death for Him, consequently, was not vanquish, but accomplishment. His foes thought they were killing Him as a common criminal. Truly, they were helping at His crowning coronation, for they were doing what the determinate counsel and foreknowledge of God had foreordained.

Jesus Christ's death was His sublimest act of submission to the awesome, divine will of God. Jesus put His foot on the summit stair of service there at Calvary. He came to do the Father's will. Jesus was doing it in every act and word and articulation of His life. In all there was perfect harmony. In any case, there at the cross was the supreme test.

The prayer of Gethsemane was all the while trembling on His lips: "Father, if it be possible, let this cup pass from me. Nevertheless, not my will, but thine, be done." Into the shadow He ran with the cry: "My God, my God, why hast thou forsaken me?" It sounds like a reverberation from the Old Testament. "Though he slay me, yet will I trust him." "This he stated, implying by what death he should to glorify God."

Jesus Christ's death was His magnificent, glorious triumph in light of the fact that by it He uncovered to men the way that God was a Father. It was this that He came to achieve. He stated: "He that hath seen me hath seen the Father." There is nothing that so glories God as this revelation not that God has power and intelligence and information and blessedness and truth, but that He is a Father.

There on the cross Jesus made the supreme disclosure of God. He dissipated the mists. He tore away the veil. He let us look fully upon the revealed face of God, and as the soul observed, it cried: "Abba Father!"

Jesus Christ's triumphant death offers back to God His wayward, meandering children. His death was the amends, the at-one-ment, the extraordinary compromise. By His stripes we are healed. His blood cleanses us from all transgression (sin). Through Christ's death the lost sinner is saved.

What a serenade ascends from the recovered crowd who have washed their robes and made them white in the blood of the Lamb, and who sing: "Glory and honor and power be unto him!" And they sing this signifying by what death He should glorify God!

The Adoration Of The Cross

THE WORLD HAS SINCE a long time ago come to worship the penal scars of the crucified Christ. Jesus Who died on Calvary is the Hero of the race. Everything looks toward him. Jesus is pioneer and Savior of humanity. His name is above each name, and His kingdom of fraternity and harmony is the dream of the country.

Jesus Christ is the world's Hero since He died,- not on the grounds that He was born in Bethlehem, not on the grounds that He lived in Nazareth as the Son of a carpenter, not on the grounds that He walked the dusty streets and ascended the harsh mountainsides and suffered with poor people and the penniless, but since He walked the winding thorn way to the cross-crowned slope, (the place of the skull) and there laid down His life.

For this we adore Him. His disciples did not attempt to shroud the way that He died. They proclaimed it. Woe to the Church should it at any point come to cloud or apologize for the death of Jesus Christ!

The cross is the image of symbol of power,- not the manger cradle, not the sunshine throne, but the cross, the blood-stained, shadowed cross on which He died. The cross crowns our church with hope. The cross waves on our Christian banner. Ahead Christians soldiers marching as to war. Also, it is the cross we wear on our souls. It is the death of Jesus Christ we praise in the communion.

The ordinance symbols speak to us not so much of the morn when the startled shepherds came nor of the night when the wise men bowed at the stable nor of great importance when the hoards thronged Him by the lakeside nor of the day He made His triumphed entry through the waving palms into Jerusalem, but of that dark hour when the sun concealed its face and the dead walked the earth and Jesus hanging between heaven and earth gave His life a ransom for many." For as often as ye eat this bread and drink this cup, ye do show the Lord's death till he come."

Let us not obscure the cross nor make little of that of which Christ makes much. Let us not fear death, not on the grounds that death is unreal, on grounds that it is real, in light of the fact that being real, Jesus Christ has tasted death for each man, and making death tell the narrative of God's love, and by making death glorious.

What is Jesus Christ's death to me? I examine His lessons, respect His model, acclaim the Sermon on the Mount, declare the kingdom of fraternity, but what is it to me that He Who said all this and did all this, Who gave the world the mystery of the new heavens and the new earth, and Who carried on with the fairest life the world has known, hung in forlornness on a cross and poured out His life unto death? What is it to me that Jesus Christ died, died for me?

Let us assemble around the cross and speak in whispers and say to our hearts: "He died for me." Let us look on the penal scars of Calvary and love Him. As we see the print of the nails let us love Him. As we see the corona on His temples and the adoration light in His face, as we eat the bread and drink the cup to show forward His death, let our hearts be singing the old tune of a green slope far away, where Jesus kicked the died

"- that we may be forgiven He died to make us good, That we may go at last to heaven, Saved by His precious blood!"

Taking Jesus Christ From The Cross

"He came therefore and took the body of Jesus."
(John 19:38)

THIS VERSE HANGS TWO pictures on the wall. The first is the image of Jesus Christ in the hands of His adversaries. They are nailing Him to the cross. The discourteous framework is outlined against the sky. To the cross on the right with overwhelming thongs they tie a thief. To the cross on the left they do in like manner.

At that point they lift the central cross from its place, and laying it down on the ground they extend their unfortunate victim on its emaciated timbers, and rather than thongs they drive the nails through His shuddering flesh. At that point, they lift the tree (cross) with it human burden, and with a jar of quickest torment they drop the cross to its place.

Jesus Christ In The Hands Of His Enemies

FOR THREE EXTENDED PERIODS Jesus Christ hung there among paradise and earth in conciliatory reparation for human blame. The rankling sun beat down on His fevered, throbbing body, until He cried: "I thirst!" The horde of sighteers passed by swaying their heads and saying: "He saved others, himself he can't save." His killers sat down before the suffering Christ, and gambling for His pieces of clothing.

Over this from the pale lips of the killed came the petition: "Father, pardon them, for they know not what they do!" And one who saw this was changed over, until over his lips, stained regularly with obscenity, passed the supplication: "Remember me!" And a Roman soldier who was a sufficient man to despise fraud and love gallantry gazed upward into Christ's face and stated: "Truly, this was the Son of God!"

At that point before long the little gathering of companions observing there out there move closer until they converse with Him and glance through spilling eyes into the face they cherish. Among them is His mother, she who held Him in her arms that wondrous night the shepherds came, who saw the praise of the Magi for her Hero Child, who noticed His each act and word amid those cheerful years at Nazareth and followed Him with her heart.

This is the deplorable end, all things considered, As they hold up there while the shadows develop about them Jesus defends the fate of His human mother as He offers her to John's consideration, saying: "Woman, Behold thy son," and afterward to John" "Behold thy mother."

Then He appears to abandon His human mother to His perfect Father, only to discover the face dismissed, until in His forlornness He cries: "My God, why hast thou forsaken me?"

Before long the well used body falls into the arms of death holding on to get it, but at that time the soul sidesteps dying, and keeping in mind that leaving His body in death's arms, Jesus Christ cries: "Father, into thy hands I commend my spirit." "And having said this, he surrendered the ghost." "It is finished."

The cost has been paid. Jesus Christ has died on the cross. Straightforwardly a Roman soldier in wanton ruthlessness will drive his lance into the dead Christ's side, and there will spill out blood blended with water. The Savior's heart was broken.

Jesus Christ In The Hands
Of His Friends

THE SECOND PICTURE IS that of Jesus Christ in the hands of His friends. They are taking Him from the cross. Who will have boldness enough for that grand dedication? He should hazard his very own life who endeavors it. He should overcome the group which early today yelled: "Crucify Him!" He should confront the despise which drove the nails into His hands.

One must endanger his position, his property, life itself, to remain by that central cross and say to Annas and Caiaphas and Pilate and Herod and the horde: "You have crucified Him, but however He be dead, I worship Him still!" Where are the individuals who will chance all to save the assemblage of Jesus Christ from a homeless person's grave?

Who will impact enough to verify consent from Christ's foes to pay such a tribute to the memory of Jesus? Without a doubt His disciples finally are prepared to die for Him; they will confront the group and say what should be said, despite the fact that it might imply that they should walk tomorrow the miserable route to their very own Calvary. In any case, they are without influence.

Should they ask Pilate for the body of Jesus, his answer would without a doubt be to order them to be imprisoned. The request must originate from a man whose standing is with the end goal that Pilate will cringe.

In this manner it was that Joseph of Arimathea is the disciple of Jesus, however subtly because of a paranoid fear of the Jews, who gets himself, and shaking off his shyness, develops away from any confining influence. In the hour of his Master's thrashing, Joseph proclaims his faith. He is rich and influential, and finally he is gallant.

He goes to Pilate and asks for the dead body of Jesus. At that point with Nicodemus, another secret disciple who had come to Jesus by night, but who is going now in the blasting day in the wild light of the impression that was clearing Jerusalem, Joseph of Arimathea goes to take Christ from the cross.

Without a doubt these two men had other of Christ's disciples to help them in this blessed ministry. Softly and affectionately they lift the dear structure from that framework of appeasement. Respectfully they plan for it for burial. At that point Joseph says: "There in my garden nursery in the midst of the sprouting blossoms under the slope is the tomb in which I had figured my very own body may rest when finally God bids me come.

The sepulchre is new. It is unsullied, for in it was man never yet laid. It disregards the valley and directions the far off slopes, and around the entryway the vines are climbing and close by the lilies before long will be in bloom. Let us lay His precious body there."

In this manner they took Jesus Christ's body from the cross and laid it in Joseph's tomb. These are the two pictures which hang before our faith,- the image of Jesus Christ in the hands of His enemies and the image of Jesus Christ in the hands of His friends.

In Which Picture?

ALL OF US IS in either of these pictures. On must take some demeanor toward Jesus Christ. He should be either for Him or Against Him, for Jesus Christ is unavoidable.

It is safe to say that we are nailing Him to the cross? The creator of the Epistle to the Hebrews discusses the individuals

Dr. John Thomas Wylie

who execute the Son of God over again. They make Calvary persistent. They draw out the execution scene and protract it out on the canvas of time. We are told who these are. They were once illuminated. They have tasted of the radiant blessing. They were made partakers of the Holy Ghost. They have tasted the great expression of God and the forces of the world to come.

Be that as it may, they have fallen far from this. They have detested and rejected the qualities there displayed, and doing as such, they execute (crucify) to themselves the Son of God over again and put Him to an open disgrace.

It was sufficiently terrible to crucify Jesus Christ the first run through, to be a Pilate, a Caiaphas, to be the soldiers who drove the nails and throw dice for His robe, to have a place with the group who gone by swaying their heads.

But, to do this now after all the light and love of two thousand years have laid on that scene is to bring about a more noteworthy judgment. Would it be able to be workable for one in this way to treat Jesus? Doubtlessly I would never nail Him to the cross, but then he that isn't for is against.

Let us pray that we might be of the company of those who took Jesus Christ from the cross. Have we enough boldness for that commitment, enough valor to confront the world and state: "This disdained and rejected man is my Savior! Give men a chance to consider Him or of me. He is my glorious Redeemer. For His dear name I will live, and should He need it, I believe I may have grace for His radiant cause to die!"

Jesus Christ would have us take Him from the cross. He has paid our obligation (debt). The sacrifice is done. The work of Calvary is finished, but not His work among men. He is to leave the cross for the road, the home, the school, the workplace, the world, and we who are His friends must take Him there.

Jesus would have us take Him from the cross, not lay Him in another impressive tomb, as I dread we once in a while envision, in some stupendous house of God or incredible church which is as a general rule a catacomb, a mausoleum. What He needs is for His people to interpret Him, His beliefs, His affection, His strength, His law of sacrifice, His compassion, and tenderness and pardoning into the life of this fatigued, sin-stricken world.

We are to take Him from the cross to the throne. He is to rule until he has put all foes under His feet. He is to establish a kingdom, to wear a crown and use a staff. The cross simply marks the way to power, and to His disciples is given the act not of entombment but of enthronement and of crowning coronation.

The Message Of The Lord's Supper

THE LORD'S SUPPER (HOLY Communion) speaks to us of the two pictures. It talks about Jesus Christ on the cross. These ordinances are the picture story of His passion. They reveal to us how He suffered. In the event that we hear them out, they will disclose to all of us that is in the first picture, of how He died. They disclose to us that He died for us that we may be forgiven, redeemed, and made the sons and daughters of the Lord God Almighty.

It likewise speaks to us of taking Jesus Christ from the cross. The message of the risen Christ was: "Go ye into all the world and preach the gospel to every creature." This, as well, is the message of the symbols (the bread and the wine or the cup). The Christ Who died must live.

Dr. John Thomas Wylie

We should preach Jesus until He lives in each man and in each land and in all the life of the world. We should put Jesus on the throne until the kingdoms of the world are His kingdoms. We should make Jesus Christ King. In the observance of the ordinance the heart that loves Jesus Christ is singing faintly: "Gracious, sacrosanct Head, when injured," but it is additionally singing in sublime expectation:

"Jesus will rule where'ver the sun does his successive journeys run."

The Human Christ

"And Jesus went forth and saw a great
multitude, and was moved with compassion
toward them, and he healed their sick."
(Matthew 14:14)

—————————

JESUS WAS EXHAUSTED WITH His work. he was endeavoring
to make tracks in an opposite direction from the crowd for a
touch of rest. His nerves were tense. He should have calm and
an opportunity to unwind from the terrible strain and expense
the persistent and thoughtless crowds made on Him.

Thus He turns His face toward the desert. Barely have
His worn out body and spent soul respected rest when there
they are. The crowds have attacked His desert. They are
disregarding His asylum, swarming about Him, clamoring to
see Him, requesting His consideration. They will give Him
no rest.

What did Jesus say? Did He issue a request to push them
away? Did He say: "These people have no thought. They are
childish. They are savage. They would have me die in my
tracks. I have done what's necessary. I am exhausted. Send
them away. Instruct them to be calm. Stop their commotion
that I may rest. Dispose of them some way or another, for I
should rest"?

Had we been in His place, it is something like this we
would have said. We have little persistence with any one who
exasperates our rest. But when exhausted with work, and with
nerves tense, one feels he has a privilege to a touch of calm.

By and by, Jesus never thought of Himself. The crowds
have broken in on His rest. How can He take it? "Also, Jesus
went forth and saw an extraordinary huge number (great

multitude), and was moved with compassion toward them, and he healed their sick."

The Compassion Of Christ

WHEN JESUS LOOKED OUT on the crowd, He saw bounty to condemn, much that wasn't right, a great deal that was childish, not somewhat that was despicable.

He saw Sabbath breakers, individuals who had no regard for the Fourth Commandment, who made the day of rest a period of pagan increase and joy. Some appear to view Sabbath defilement as a cutting edge wrongdoing. It is the most old of transgressions.

He saw individuals who did not hesitate to cheat and lie so as to profit, who cheated, who profiteered, who were not willing to pay their legit obligations, who were blameworthy of trickery and rascality. These things went on in past times worth remembering that are no more.

He saw degenerate government officials. We think some about the political arrangements of our day register the last demonstration in the disloyalty of an open trust, however present day governmental issues is a Sunday school issue in examination with what went on in Jesus Christ's time.

He saw experience. He saw the vain show. He saw individuals who sat down to eat and to drink, and who ascended to play. He saw the revel of Bacchus and the uproar of passion. It was a day when a young lady won as her trophy the dribbling head of John the Baptist, when the custom of religion comprised in the act of the ceremonies of the goddess of lust.

He saw bad faith (hypocrisy). He saw men wearing the uniform of paradise to serve the demon in. He saw guile

Dr. John Thomas Wylie

devoutly veneering itself, and frauds holing up behind the skirts of clerics, and hands stained with wrongdoing serving at the altar, and lips foul with impiety discussing the statement of faith. He saw a lot to censure. In any case, interestingly, no analysis tumbled from His lips.

He was moved with compassion. He was touched with pity. He was loaded up with a bitterness that occasionally could convey what needs be only in tears. The transgression of the world did not make Him bitter.

Jesus Christ was not biting. The only things which blended Him to outrage and revilement were dogmatism and false reverence. Indeed, even these did not lead Him to assemble His articles of clothing about Him with a "holier-than-thou" frame of mind to life and pull back from the crowd. Rather than moving back, He pushed in where the crowd was, directly into the thick of filthy and stained and defeated humankind.

This does not imply that He was tolerant toward transgression. How might He be? He came to battle it, to incapacitate it of its power, to destroy its hold on human life, to pass on Himself on the detestable cross that He may lift from its exploited people the scourge of wrongdoing. One doesn't comprehend the compassion of Jesus who supposes it implies a pale ethical quality. Jesus Christ was immaculate. With Him, blessedness was a passion. The forsaken Christ was brutal toward wrongdoing.

In any case, He was understanding with the sinner. He recognized sin and the sinner. It is a refinement we once in a while neglect to make, and fizzling, we wind up basic and hypercritical rather than humane. We remain off with a pretentious air and convey ourselves of a melancholy jeremiad of our occasions, of a harsh tirade against our kindred men, of a furious impugning of the transgressions and deficiencies of Sabbath breakers and profiteers, of grafters and experience and wolves in sheep's clothing.

The outcome is, we leave the sin sick world as sin sick and miserable and sad as we discovered it. It was not so with Jesus. He saw an extraordinary huge number(a great multitude) and was moved with compassion.

Jesus, The Helping Christ

JESUS HELPED PEOPLE SINCE He had compassion on them. This was His strategy for treatment. It was His solution for a broken and edgy and hopeless world. He directed patience and love. Read the Gospel story. Presently He sees the people as sheep not having a shepherd, and He has compassion.

Presently it is a leper, shunned from his kind, and He has compassion. There two visually impaired (blind) men are sobbing for benevolence, for mercy and He has compassion. Here is a stained young lady from the streets, and Jesus sees her and has compassion on her.

He has compassion since He finds in each sinner God's child, alienated, wayward, lost, but at the same time with the tracery of the Father there. He finds in each rich man Zaccheus, a potential altruist. He sees in working men what He found in the anglers of Galilee, witnesses, evangelists, world developers. He found in the beset demoniac of the tomb not the poor creature to be sent to a crazy refuge, however an individual to be liberated, and who, when dressed and in his right mind, was to wind up a witness for his Redeemer.

He found in the young lady of the street not an outcast to be stoned by society's cold and hardhearted crowd, but one who may turn into an angel of mercy.

Dr. John Thomas Wylie

He found in the cheat (thief) on the cross a native of Heaven. This He saw since He was moved with compassion.

Jesus saw this godlike side of life being overlooked, quelled, scorned, impeded, banished, crushed. This is the thing that disheartened Him. What's more, He saw that the best approach to discharge it and to empower it to pick up the ascendency in the soul was not to turn upon it the wild rage or wrath of God, but to gather it with delicate, gentle love.

Consequently as Jesus moved among men, He accomplished more than reprimand them, more than censure. Jesus had compassion on them, and saved them. He Helped them to find themselves and become the sons and daughters of their Heavenly Father.

The Human Christ

JESUS HAD COMPASSION BECAUSE He was human. At first become flushed this announcement might be tested, but reflection will vindicate it. Jesus was "tempted in all points like as we are." He was broadly human. His experience cleared the entire array of human life. He can be touched with the sentiment of our illnesses. He can feel as we feel, and feeling therefore, He has compassion. This is the great lesson of the incarnation. It is godhood becoming human.

It isn't the godhood getting to be severe and denunciatory, but human. I was talking one day with a Jew who had acknowledged Christ in one of our gatherings. He was depicting how Christ engaged him. He stated: "Jesus has humanized the religion of the Old Testament." It appeared to me a fine portrayal of the motivation behind the manifestation.

Jesus did not found another religion, but He humanized the religion of the Old Testament. A few people are living back there. They are hard, hard as Sinai. Jesus did not nullify the moral law, however He humanized it. He said: "Love is the fulfilling of the law."

Thus, as He watches out on the crowd, Jesus sees people, not the huge number, however people and children, not social units, but fathers and mothers and married couples and brothers and sisters and neighbors and companions. Jesus singles us out of the crowd.

He sees the elderly person moving with moderate advance down life's last slope, and feels for his frame of mind to life. Jesus sees the mother murmuring over a child in her arms, and comprehends her longing and hope.

Jesus sees the father as he bids a fond farewell to the son who is leaving home, and knows such assembles around that separating. Jesus sees the worker as he leaves for his work in the first part of the day, and enters with him into his day of drudge. He sees the criminal behind the bars, and goes into compassion for him. What's more, since Jesus sees this, not simply human advancement and laws and countries, but people, He has feel sorry for them, out of His compassion.

Jesus sees this since He is so human. His humanity is huge, high, wide, vast, delicate. Here is the incredible verification of His godhood. There are those, maybe, who believe in Jesus as a result of His miracles. I have faith in the miracles because of Jesus. Christ is the best contention for Christianity. When He asked Peter: "Whom do men say that I the Son of Man am?" Peter answered: "Son of God!"

He appears to state: "Thou art so human, Thy humanity is so huge, so racial, so great, so comprehensive, that Thou art more than Son of Man: Thou art God!"

It is this delicate, human Christ Who comes to meet us as we gather around the communion table. He would sit with us here at the Lord's Supper. He would be as well disposed with us similarly as with that little gathering of disciples the evening of the first dinner. He is our Redeemer, but He is our Elder Brother, as well. He is our Upper Room friend, our closes friend and always with us.

There are a great deal of desolate individuals on the planet, and maybe in light of the fact that they are forlorn, some of them are terrible. God made us to be social creatures. Isolation is damnation. The reckless achieved the profundities when "no man gave unto him." Some one has illustrated two polar bears on a field of ice.

One of the bears is dead, starved to death in the distressing Arctic world, and his mate remains next to him looking down with an articulation, but rather of dread of torment. The craftsman calls his image "Isolation."

When one feels that none is left to mind, it is a solidified world, and there is not all that much however demise. What individuals need today is fellowship and compassion. It is the human Christ Who recuperates the damages of mankind, and He mends them by being human. It is divine to be human.

The Divine Christ

"Who being in the form of God, thought it
not robbery to be equal with God."
(Philippians 2:6)

———————

"DIVINITY" HAS BEEN EXTRAORDINARILY ruined. There
are those individuals who concede the eternality of Christ,
however who deny His divinity. There are the individuals who
concede that Christ is divine, however who guarantee that
man is divine. If Christ is divine just as we may be, He was a
decent man, however no more, and He has no more case on
our remembrance than a huge number of other people who
have loved and served and suffered and died. It is God we
remember at the Holy Communion, we called it: "The Lord's
Supper."

Laying Aside His GodHood

———————

BUT THEN CHRIST'S FIRST go about as the world's Redeemer
was to lay His godhead aside. It is an abnormal and capturing
thing said by Paul in his letter to the Philippians; in talking
about Christ, he pronounces: "Who being in the form of God,
thought it not robbery to be equal with God." The American
update deciphers it: "Being on an equality with God." And
Dr. Moffatt utilizes the brilliant expression: "Though He was
divine by nature, He didn't snatch at equality with God, but
emptied Himself."

These interpretations, in any case, are nevertheless unique
methods for saying that in His natural service Jesus purposely
laid His godhead aside. He didn't draw on His divine powers

to secure and support Himself amid the time of His temptation and suffering. His human experience was genuine, it was real.

His misery on the cross was real. Jesus was not a performing artist having an impact. He was a self-chosen sufferer vicariously bearing the punishment of transgression for mankind.

Because He laid His godhead aside in confronting His passion, we are not to infer that He had any uncertainty about His deity. He was sure of that that He could stand to empty Himself. Nor are we to conclude in any sense He ceased to be God. How right? One can avoid practicing certain forces which he has, however he doesn't in this way stop to act naturally, or be himself.

Nor does it imply that He didn't exercise these powers for other people. For sure it was only this Christ did in His heavenly nature, and this established the poignancy and magnificence of His ministry.

He fed the hoards, however declined to transform one stone to bread to end His very own fast. He healed the injuries of others, but He would not staunch His own. He raised Lazarus from the dead, however He declined to protect Himself against death. This course was not accidental. It was deliberate, intentional. Christ was not a victim. He was a victor.

Thus this unusual line presenting the plummet of a God into the Valley of humiliation does not stop with the descent. It also drones His climb toward the statures of exaltation. Surely, when we see aright Christ plunge, it was itself an ascend. Jesus was none the less God in the valley than on the heights.

The human Christ being so substantially, so transcendantly human, could be none other than the divine Christ. Thus Paul paints the two representations. "Who being as God, thought it not robbery to be equal with God, but made himself of no

Dr. John Thomas Wylie

reputation, and took upon him the form of a servant, and was made in the likeness of men, and being found in fashion as a man, he humbled himself and became obedient unto death, even the death of the cross."

"Wherefore God hath still highly exalted him and given him a name which is above every name, that at the name of Jesus every knee should bow, of things in heaven, and things in earth, and things under the earth, and that each tongue should confess that Jesus Christ is Lord to the glory of God the Father."

Recognizing His Godhood

THE GODHOOD OF JESUS isn't something for us to dismiss. Maybe somebody may ask: "How would you know that Jesus is God?" I may reply: "I trust and I believe it. I believe a few things I do not know. My faith is that Jesus is divine as well as human. We consider Him the "God-Man," (100% God, 100% Man). Be that as it may, if this faith isn't to be censured as credulity, it must demonstrate its sensibility. I figure it can."

I believe in the godhead of Jesus due to the teachings of the Bible. It once in a while is said that the Bible does not say in any place that Jesus is God. One may concede that the Bible does not contend the god of Jesus Christ. It assumes it. It underestimates it (takes for granted), and in specific passages, similar to the prelude to John's Gospel, it proclaims it in the clearest and most undeniable language.

The Bible is dependable, trustworthy. It has been attempted and tried and pounced upon as no other book, and it has left all contentions triumphant. Will we decay to acknowledge its declaration? Will we acknowledge what satisfies us and reject of the Book what we despise?

Will we acknowledge what it says about the human Christ and reject what it says about the divine Christ? You can not treat the Bible that way. You can not guarantee what suits you and deny what bothers you.

I believe in the godhead of Jesus Christ since He said things which only God has an option to state. "I am the way, the truth, and the life." "I and my Father are one." "I am the bread of life." "If ye abide in me and my words abide in you, you shall ask what ye will and it will be done unto you."

These words don't sit well on the lips of a mere man, If Jesus is God, they are what we would anticipate that Him should say.

I believe in His deity because He did things which only God has power to do. Jesus worked miracles. Jesus healed illness. Jesus cast out devils. Jesus raised the dead. Jesus became alive once again. One may said he did this since He had a profounder understanding into the working of nature's laws. Most likely there is quite a bit of truth in the statement.

If we comprehended what Jesus knew we may do numerous things He did. What's more, we may locate that much which presently appears to be phenomenal was only the working out of higher laws. In any case, is it not abnormal that Jesus was the only man with this knowledge? How did that peasant Jew, unlettered back in that dim age, gain this knowledge?

Where was ever a school that could teach what Jesus knew? It charges faith more to trust that He was an unimportant man who did this than it does to have faith in His deity.

I have faith in His godhood in light of the fact that no other man has ever been what Jesus was. Jesus is confessed to be the one perfect man in mankind's history. There was an ethical glory about His character that has never been coordinated. He towers high over the various educators. He had a major and personal comprehension of human nature.

In the most commonplace land and of a most common race, He Himself was cosmopolitan. He had a self-destruction that is the surrender all expectations regarding others. In the event that He is just human, for what reason would he say he is the only human to be this? For what reason would we say we are not developing other men greater and better? I have faith in His godhead since He is unmatched among men.

This, yet Jesus is doing what no other man can do. He died on the cross two thousand years back and was buried, however in His name men leave all, suffer, all, endeavor all. Through faith in Him the world is improving. Heathens are evolving.

Human nature is regenerated. Distress is helped, comforted. Cataclysm is gallantly confronted. Thrashing is changed to triumph. For what reason are not other men ready to motivate this in their followers?

Mohammed, Confucius, Buddha, have left a dead world in their trail, but Jesus Christ is the light and life of men.

Isn't this enough to vindicate one's faith against a charge of credulity when he respectfully pronounces: "I believe that Jesus is God!" But this isn't all. There comes when the individuals who do His will can say: "I know whom I have believed." I am as sure of the godhood of Jesus Christ as I am of any reality not powerless of scientific exhibition. I realize He is God through Christian experience. This is the most noteworthy certitude. The faculties may beguile us, the soul, never.

The contention for the divinity of Christ is basic. It is possible that He is God or He isn't. In the event that He isn't, He was either beguiled about Himself or He was misdirecting others about Himself. He was either rationally lopsided or an impostor. Nobody who examines the teachings of Jesus can acknowledge both of those options.

Jesus Christ is God. Be that as it may, the spirit needs more than contention. It needs conviction, assurance and confirmation, and these come not as the result of a psychological procedure but rather of a life experience.

Claiming His Godhood

THE GODHOOD OF JESUS is something to claim. Let us not be so caught up with endeavoring to demonstrate that Jesus is God that we will neglect to suitable the radiant truth. The Bible does not endeavor to demonstrate that Jesus is God. It fabulously continues on the reason of His deity.

On the last extraordinary day of the banquet Jesus stood and stated: "If any man thirst, let him come to me and drink." He would have us approach Him, remember Him that He is very God and bounteously ready to supply every one of our needs.

Truly! Jesus is God, He can and will stay faithful to His commitments. We can count on them. All that He teach is true. All that He said about God and the great beyond is reliable. If He is only a man, He might be mixed up, however, If He is God, there is assurance.

If Jesus is God, He can save us. He can forgive our wrongdoings (sins) and change our inclinations. He can give us power to become the children of God. He can endorse predetermination. In the event that He is only a man, His impact is dubious, however on the off chance that God, He is the compelling Redeemer.

In the event that Jesus is God, His motivation will triumph. Nothing can crush it. The world will come His direction. In reality, it is coming His direction. Gradually but without a doubt progress is being built as per His lessons.

In the event that Jesus is only a man, there is no more trust in the triumph of His lessons than for those of some other great man, however, If He be God, His motivation is planned for triumph, and against it the doors of hellfire will not win.

Why not guarantee the godhood of Christ and make it a piece of your life? There is nothing to lose, however such a great amount to pick up. It is smarter to have a great Christ than a little one. Imagine a scenario in which there are questions. Is it worse to pursue faith than questions? If one is to take risks in any case, is it worse to take them in favor of our expectations than of our apprehensions?

There is no attracting force a nullification. There is no lifting and moving force in a refusal. What the world needs isn't refutations, however positions. Society has nothing to fear from faith in the divinity of Christ. Maybe somebody may state that it has nothing to fear from a forswearing of His divinity. But, makes them anything to trust from such refusal?

There can be no desires from a clique that connects with to accomplish for one just what he can accomplish for himself. The heathen (sinner) needs a Savior who has power, who can reach down and lift up, who can change the individual, who can save unto the furthest. Such is Jesus!

"Of Me"

"...this do in remembrance of me."
(Luke 22:19)

JESUS SAYS: "THIS DO in remembrance of me." He asserts our consideration. He appears to say: "I need you to be caught up with me, not with musings of yourselves, of your congregation, of your minister and his message, but of me." He doesn't state that He needs us to remember something about Him, to review His words, His work, His sufferings.

Obviously there is a sense in which all these group in as we consider Him. In any case, He is more than any lesson He at any point preached or taught, or any supernatural occurrence (miracle) He ever created, and He says: "Remember me." The identity of Christ is the image on which faith is to dwell in the ordinance.

The Egotism Of Jesus

JESUS WAS THE BEST egotist the world has ever known. One needs but to review a portion of His lessons to be persuaded of this. He stated: "Whosoever believeth in me will be saved." He dismisses all others as fakers, and cases that He, and only he, is Savior.

He says: "I am the way, the truth and the life. No man cometh unto the Father but by me." He sends all frameworks and statements of faith and associations and religions to the back, and fills their places with Himself. He promises that He, and only he, has the power to introduce men to God. He is the only way, and he that climbeth up some other way is a criminal and a looter.

Hear Him as He brings the world into His heart, and says: "Come unto me, all ye that work and are substantial loaded, and I will give you rest." Recite the travail of the world. Think about its torment and misery, of its regret and severe frustration, of all its distress and tears. In what manner can such ailment ever be healed?

For Jesus Christ it is simple. He says: "Simply come to me, and your tired hearts will be cured." He accept the power to forgive sin. He says: "The Son of Man hath power on earth to forgive sin." He is promising blameless flawlessness, for He pardons sin, He doesn't commit it. He asks: "Lovest thou me?" and makes dedication to Himself the incomparable rationale (supreme motive) in Christian service.

Christianity is the religion of a Person,- not of a custom or a clique or a framework, but of a Person. People are religious not as they are universal, not as they recount an ordinance, not as they release certain obligations and buy in to specific perspectives, however as they are identified with Jesus Christ.

Then Jesus Christ is more than a mere man. It would be sacrilege for a simple man to state what Christ says. It would be more terrible than a sham for the best of men to guarantee what Christ claims. It would be more than strange for them to maintain to do what Jesus Christ does. Be that as it may, He performs what He proposes. His promises merit their presumptive worth. Jesus Christ makes good.

His is the self love of a God. It doesn't irritate us. It would be unusual if, being what He will be, He should state less. Jesus accepted His godhood. He didn't guarantee it, in light of the fact that such case was superfluous. In so far as saving Himself went, He discharged (emptied) Himself of His godhood, since He came to carry on with a genuine human life, to meet preliminary as we should meet it, and to be enticed in all points like as we may be. In any case, let us not misjudge Him. This does not imply that Jesus Christ takes a second place.

The Goal Of Religion

JESUS IS THE GOAL of religion. Jesus comes first. He is the chiefest among ten thousand and the one through and through lovely. Maybe you are attempting to be religious. What do you mean by it? What thought is in your psyche and what plan would you say you are following to achieve your longing? You go to chapel, however why? You contribute your cash to great aims, however why?

To whom would you say you are making your blessings? To the congregation? To mankind? Maybe you encourage a class in the Sunday school, or help at the mission, or are a worker at a sanctuary. For whom would you say you are doing this? Investigate your religion. Maybe quite a bit of it never gets to Jesus Christ by any stretch of the imagination.

A significant number of the things we do we do essentially in light of the fact that we like to do them. The administration is amicable. Maybe it makes us feel critical. It arranges us with individuals who are better than average and liberal and decent. We are enamored with the congregation. We need to make a decent record. We might want to meet the desires which the world has of us. Society may call us mean were we to decline. And the majority of this is commendable and nice, as it were, but it isn't being a Christian. An agnostic can go this far.

Christ says: "I need you to do it for me. When you help a faltering man, I need you to think not such a large amount of him, but of me. When you are occupied with Christian service, I would have your mind loaded up with musings less of the congregation or of the class as of me. When you give your cash, back of the blessing I would have you recall not only the community or the heathen, or even my servant the minister, however I need you to remember me, your Savior."

Does Christ emerge before us? Is it accurate to say that he is supreme? Have we felt that what we were doing, we were accomplishing for Him, and that when we neglected to do, it was not the general people we harmed, nor the congregation, but were driving the nails into the hands of Christ? Have you at any point heard Him shout out as you pushed down the thorns? No. His lips express no word.

However, in the event that we could see the inconspicuous, we may perceive what Peter saw that night at the preliminary when, as he denied Him, he turned and saw Jesus. We may hear what John heard as He tuned in to his Master that horrendous night before Pilate.

Give us a chance to correct our intentions here at the communion table. What is the place we give Jesus Christ? In our extraordinary battles for the kingdom, what intention drives us on? Is it church pride, or denominational devotion, or the respect that connects to progress, or is it only for Him?

"This do in remembrance of me." That will sustain us. It will make the troublesome simple. It will keep us sweet when we are enticed to be unpleasant. It will empower us to see the best in others, and it will empower us to cheer in torment. I have known about a young fellow who came to American from a country to whom we send evangelists, missionaries. He had known about Jesus, and had figured out how to cherish Him. He needed to fit himself for Christian support of his own country.

Without methods, he was working his entry in the smothering hold of the ship as a stoker, however he said what sustained him was, amidst the terrible warmth and soil of that long passage, that it was for Jesus Christ.

It is our devotion to Jesus that will shape the decision finally. "I was in jail and ye came unto me." Maybe we were not constantly cognizant that He was there, however it was not for the detainee, it was for the Christ that we went. It was in His name that we gave some water to a parched disciple. It was on the grounds that we knew and loved Jesus Christ that we gave a lift to the hurt man on the roadway, and the Judge is stating" "Because of the fact that ye did it unto a standout amongst the least if these, my brethren, ye did it unto me."

"This do in remembrance of me." May we consider Him to be we Father around the communion table. In the heavenly quiet of communion, for us may it be Jesus Christ, only Jesus. Come, Lord Jesus, come quickly!"

The Program Of
The Upper Room

"Ye are witnesses of these things."
(Luke 24:48)

THE PLACE WAS THE Upper room at Jerusalem. It was the first house of God of the Christian Church. There was no raised area, no choir, no nave, no cross. It was without Gothic curves and steepled splendor. There were only the four exposed walls of a typical room, but there never was assembled a house that held a greater amount of God than that plain Upper room.

It was where the Holy Communion (The Lord's Supper) was established, where Jesus Christ's followers made their home after they had lost their Master. It was the room in which the prayer meeting was held which went before Pentecost, when the Holy Spirit plunged in power and the endowment of tongues was offered. There more than once the risen Christ showed Himself to His friends. Such is the place.

The people in this room comprise of Jesus Christ and ten men, Thomas the doubter was absent. They are the friends who had followed Christ the three unusual and significant long years of His natural service, but circumstances are different. They have seen Him captured and crucified.

They have watched Him stumble not far off under the heap of a cross. They have seen the soldiers nail Him to the tree (cross), and have heard His cries from the cross. They have watched Him die, and they have laid His body in the tomb. However, here He is with them once more. He is risen. They can't question it. He shows to them the print of the nails. He eats with them. Their Master has returned. Also, those men all tremble with the rapture of great importance.

The two disciples who saw Him in the breaking of the bread at Emmaus have told their bizarre story, and even while they let it know, Jesus is there in the upper room live with them once more, with the old look in His face, and the voice they cherish so well has yet again spoken harmony. That has excited them. What care they now for the incredible antagonistic world whose tides of unbelief and abuse break and beat outside?

The door is closed, and inside is Jesus Christ. What care they for the fighters and the clerics and the energized crowd? The world may cry: "Crucify Him!" They may nail Him to the cross and seal His mausoleum and station a soldier to guard, however they can't keep Jesus Christ in the tomb. What do these friends of Jesus Christ care now for the world?

But they should care. This is their central goal. They should think about the chilly, unfriendly, oppressing world. Alongside their Lord, there is nothing they should think about to such an extent. They should not like themselves. They should not like straightforwardness or harmony or bliss, nor tally life dear. They should hold all shabby, that they may favor the world God loved and Jesus Christ came to save.

Thus the mystical must wind up practical. The rapture must make an interpretation of itself into service. Privilege must pack itself into power. This is the law of the kingdom. It was so with the demoniac safeguarded from the tomb. It was the motivation behind that great experience on the Mount of Transfiguration.

It was the message to Mary in the greenhouse that Easter morning. What's more, it is the message here in the upper room. The poor world holds up outside the door and they must plan to save the lost. There are rooms in which the fate of countries is chosen, and the map of earth changed. There in the upper room it was the predetermination of a race that was included.

How is the world to be saved? What will be the program? In what manner will the campaign be arranged? Jesus Christ is leaving, but His work must go on. There in that upper room is to be planned the plan which is to issue in world redemption.

From the upper room is to go forward the power which is to change the world. Through that doorway straightforwardly will pass a power manifested in the identities of eleven men that will shake down each oppression, end each oppression, topple the hindrances of loathe, clear out each line of standing, fix each twisted, comfort each distress, and give sacrifice, atone for every sin.

It is a marvelous endeavor. The world is to crown Jesus Christ King. The cross must triumph. The Sermon on the Mount must be converted into training. It implies the mightiest change in mankind's history. The powers of underhandedness are to be directed, and development is to be based on the Golden Rule. This is the assignment. As of now it has in part been cultivated. All the program of world proselytizing is potential in that upper room where ten men dawdle under the spell of a resurrected Christ.

Jesus Christ declared the program. He sums it up in a solitary line.

"Ye are witnesses of these things." That was all. They were to document out of that room into the world and progress toward becoming witness. Nothing could be progressively down to earth. They were to interpret the mysterious. They were to tackle the rapture. They were to experience the harmony.

What's more, they did. In the dark first light of the day of service they opened the door of the upper room and permitted the tides of the threatening scene to break over them. They confronted the battle line and gave their declaration. They set out their lives. Be that as it may, it was victory.

Witnesses

THE PROGRAM OF THE upper room is for Jesus Christ's disciples to be witnesses. It is for the those who have sat at Jesus' feet and have learned of Him to tell what they have learned. It is for those who have heard it to distribute the uplifting news. It is for those who have progressed toward becoming partakers of the Gospel to broadcast and proclaim the message. That is all. Would anything be able to be less complex? Men were to be saved by accepting and believing. Be that as it may, how might they believe on Him of Whom they have not heard?

The program of the upper room was not for the disciples to raise a military and unsheath the sword and request to constrain. No politically influential nation is referenced. There isn't a word about cash or grant or influence or place. They had none of this. They were simply to be witnesses.

The program was not that they ought to go forward to answer the contentions of their adversaries or to answer to the analysis of those who questioned or scorned their call. They were not requested to explain away the challenges nor to mollify the hardships associated with apprenticeship. They were to be neither judge nor jury nor advocate, but just witnesses.

They were not requested to compose themselves into an organization so as to take the necessary steps. They were not advised to establish a church. Obviously, the church would come. Be that as it may, it would come as a result of witnessing. Nothing is said about a chain of importance or a brotherhood. Numerous things have been added to the program since that hour in the upper room, some of which are helpful, however in the first there was only witnessing.

It appear to be excessively basic. It sounded deficient. It looked as if the arrangement were destined to disappointment.

What did the world care for witnesses? It would detest them and indict them and quietness them. It would stomp on their declaration and proclamation. It would stack deride on their endeavors. The world would not tune in. Yet, Jesus Christ does not amend. He says: "Ye are witnesses of these things." Furthermore, He gives it a chance to remain at that. On this He stakes His motivation.

He went into battle with neither armed force nor ammo nor hardware, with eleven men for His disciples, who had nothing on the planet except for the story of their faith in their Leader.

This is as yet the program. Since that night long prior in the upper room, we have gotten a lot together. Earth is loaded up with great places of worship. The Church is rich and educated and powerful. The premier countries of the world call themselves Christian. However these are not the things that succeed. The program of triumph, of victory is as yet the program of the upper room.

The world is saved only as Jesus Christ's followers become His witnesses. It is here the tide turns.

This is all Jesus Christ asks of us, and nothing can have its place. "Ye are witnesses of these things."

The imperative thing is to be a witness. I might be a church member, yet I am not a witness, I am a disappointment. The enormous thing isn't my category, my commitment, my exercises, my insight into religious philosophy, nor theological insight, my position in the church or in the world, but my testimony. Has the world at any point thought enough about my religious life to call me to the witness stand?

The Assets Of A Witness

To be a witness one must have an experience. He should recognize what he knows. It isn't sufficient for him to realize what another person knows. It won't respond in due order regarding him to report what others state they have heard or seen or felt. He should himself have seen and heard and felt. He should know Jesus in the forgiveness of his sins.

It has been said that a man may hold office in the church. He might be a liberal giver of his means. He may discovered foundations and philanthropies and bolster a missionary. He may teach in the Sunday school.

He may do any number of beneficial things. However, he can't get into the program of the upper room. To do that, he should have an experience. He should be converted himself and be able to say: "I know!"

His testimony must be explicit. It isn't sufficient for him to tell where he lives, to declare his nationality, his condition. It won't do the trick for him to inform what he knows concerning science or lawmaking. The mission of the Church is unequivocal. The kingdom isn't meat and drink. It's anything but a monetary heaven that Jesus came to build up.

The Church isn't requested to give its testimony on each new swell that appears on the ocean of human life. It is to enlighten what it know regarding Jesus Christ, of His saving power, of His power to cure sin.

If our testimony is to be sound, our character must be in harmony with the truth we preach. It must ensure that we are dependable. A witness must be faithful. This is preeminently true with regards to religion. We should be what we proclaim. We should possess, and not merely profess. Jesus Christ's stamp must be on us. The world won't tune in to a wolf in sheep's clothing or a faker, a hypocrite or a pretender.

The Evidence

WE ARE WITNESSES OF "these things." What things? They are the things referenced in the forty-sixth and forty-seventh verse of the chapter. They are three in number.

We are to testify for the sufferings of Jesus Christ. This is the first thing the world needs to know. It must learn that He suffered. It must stop at the cross. It must find that He laid down His life for sinners. We are to go on the witness stand to prove that Calvary is a reality. How?

Not by saying, but by being. We should experience the cross. Paul declared that he filled up the sufferings of Christ, and that he bore in his body the signs of the Lord Jesus. Whatever happened to Jesus Christ must happen to His disciples. We should take up our cross and follow Him. We should be crucified with Him. Actions speak louder than words. Talk is cheap. It persuades nobody. In any case, to experience the cross,- that is unanswerable.

We must testify to the resurrection of Jesus Christ. The world also has to learn that Jesus Christ rose from the dead. This is the seal and confirmation of all He instructed. It was the great occasion. How are we to testify to the resurrection? We should do more than state that He rose.

It isn't sufficient to sing an Easter tune or hold an Easter service. Jesus Christ must be risen in us. The soul must rise up out of the tomb of transgression and narrow-mindedness. We must experience the resurrection. That was the magnificent thing about the lady who broke her alabaster box on Jesus

Christ. She was risen. The world listens less to our melody but rather more to us. If Jesus Christ is risen in me the hope of glory, that is proof.

We should testify to repentance and remission of sins in His name. This is the uplifting news, the good news the world is hanging tight to get notification from those men who are issuing from the upper room. They were not holding on to become familiar with some new hypothesis of science or the most recent securities exchange citations or the best technique for taking care of the social wickedness, but how sin could be relieved (cured) and a passage made into the kingdom of righteousness and peace and joy in the Holy Ghost.

How were they to outfit such testimony? It was insufficient to trust it or believe for themselves. They must believe it and experience it, but they must likewise proclaim it. They must see that everyone hears it. They must go into all the world and preach the Gospel to every creature. They must progress toward becoming messengers, envoys, heralds, ambassadors, living incarnations of the blessed evangel, Jesus Christ.

The Campaign

SUCH WAS THE PROGRAM of the upper room. As that little missional apostolic gathering go out, this is the thing that they went to do. After Pentecost, they started to preach,- not a system, not a creed, but evidence. They testified for the thing they knew. As they did as such the hindrances fell away and the cross was triumphant.

This is our business as Christians. The communion will help us to remember this. In our creative imagination we come back to the upper room, and there the old program welcomes us. We are witnesses of these things, in our own town, in our own home. In the workplace, the production line, in the city, on the green, in our social entertainments, in our business relations, wherever we will be, we are to be witnesses.

Jesus Christ has left His work with us. His cause stands or falls, wins or comes up short, with our testimony. The world judges the Savior by us. It's anything but an instance of the inspiration of the Bible or of the supernatural occurrences (miracles), or of the Church. It is a case of the Christian, of whether he is a positive or negative witness.

It is extraordinary to be faithful. Presently we are in the upper room. Tomorrow we will be in the world and the salvation of the world will rely upon us. It is a gigantic duty. It is an unthinkable errand that is alloted us. It tosses us back on God. With Him the incomprehensible ends up conceivable. Goodness, to catch the spirit of those men in the upper room, and of Jesus Christ's true friends who in every age have turned the tide!

Inside The Cup

"For this is my blood of the new testament, which
is shed for many for the remission of sins."
(Matthew 26:28)

───────────

By "inside the cup" I mean the contents of the communion cup which Jesus Christ grasped that game changing night in the uppe room, as He blessed the cup and passed it to His disciples, saying: "Drink ye all of it." What did Jesus Christ mean? What was inside the cup.

There was some passover wine made of the grapes which had matured on the slope there in the summer sun. Regardless of whether it was matured or unfermented wine we are not told. Contentions have seethed around the inquiry. Books have been composed regarding the matter. It isn't, be that as it may, an issue of moderately extraordinary significance.

There are some so worried for the wine in the cup that they would have none of the ordinance symbol left unused in case there ought to be the blasphemy of a sacred thing. This, as well, is likewise an issue not basic. Had it been, Christ would presumably have charged His disciples to such alert at the institution of the Supper.

The Savior's atonement was inside the cup. We are coming to something unfathomably imperative at this point. "For this is my blood of the new testament which is shed for many for the remission of sins." He was discussing His Passion.. The wine symbolizes the blood shed on the cross. The cup is the memorial of His sufferings and death.

It is the cup of sacrifice, the chalice of forgiveness, the goblet of redemption. It is this that He holds out to those men at the communion table, as He passes the cup. Let us a think about this as we commune. As we touch our lips to the cup, we are looking down on the Savior Who died that we may be forgiven, Whose blood was shed for the remission of sins, in Whose blood the travelers has wash their robes and make them white; "however our transgressions be as scarlet, they will be as white as snow."

But, this isn't all that is inside the cup. Those for whom Christ died are there. What number of are there, and of what classes? Who was Jesus Christ pondering when He said His blood was shed for many? Did He intend to incorporate just the church people, the great, the commendable, the refined and the good?

He didn't stop with these on other events. For what reason would it be a good idea for him to limit Himself here? There are homeless people inside the cup. The untouchables (lepers) are there, the weak, the lame, the halt, and the visually impaired. Take a look at them. They are moving around inside the cup. They are lifting wan faces. They are holding up their hands. They are making prayers. For Jesus Christ came to call not the upright, however sinners, to repentance, and He said: "Other sheep I have which are not of this fold."

He says that His blood was shed for many. Why not for all? What a magnificent thing in the event that He had said all! I think He wanted to say it, but He realized that some would reject it. Maybe He was thinking of Judas. He can't state all, however He says many. He implies that all who come will be received.

There is enough for all, and He can save unto the uttermost all who come unto God through Him. Be that as it may, some will decline to come. They will reject themselves. It is bizarre that they should, yet consistently we see them doing this. However the "many" stays in the line. Broaden out Christ's expression. There is a large number no man can number.

Inside the cup are some from all countries. Jesus Christ has an electorate from each nationality. His humanity is racial. He is the longing of countries. Just in Him is discovered what each country wants to figure it out. Goodness, that they could see it! What America needs is Jesus Christ. What China and Japan need is Jesus Christ. What the white man, yellow man, and black man need is the Son of Man, Jesus Christ. "I shall be satisfied when I awake in thy likeness."

This is the reason He stated: "Go ye into all the world and preach the gospel to each creature." He was thinking about every one of them when He said it, of high and low, rich and poor, publican and miscreant, disturbed and failing. He was thinking about the criminal and the street walker, presidents, kings and queens. All are there inside the cup.

It is the world's melting pot. There in the communion cup our common humanity blends, in light of the fact that there our Friend meets us. He died for all, and calls every one of us His friends. He says: "All ye are brethren."

Would it be able to be that we have retained the cup from any whom Jesus Christ set inside? If they are to find Him, they should initially know Him. By what means will they believe in Him of Whom they have not heard, and in what manner will they hear without a preacher? Have we neglected to make Him known? Have we kept out some whom Jesus Christ needs access, for whom He died, some who have as much in that place as we, some for whom He is pausing, holding on to give them remission of sins, however they have not received it in light of the fact that the knowledge has halted in us?

Give us a chance to consider them we come to communion. Give us a chance to consider him and of our high benefits in Him. It is an honored thing to sit at the table and ruminate over His wondrous love. Be that as it may, I wonder if, as He looks downward on us, He may not be thinking about some who are not His? He misses them. Some are not here in light of the fact that they never got an opportunity.

They got no opportunity since some who knew neglected to tell them that there is room, and that they are expected. It is weird that we ought to overlook at the table where the one thing He asks is that we recall.

The communion was being observed in a great church. The symbols had been passed. Following a custom here and there rehearsed, the preacher was asking: "Have any been omitted?" And a lady who had communed said she couldn't help thinking that as she heard the inquiry, many ladies started to emerge from the nations of the earth, from China, and Africa, and India, and Korea, and Japan, and as they stood up, they appeared to shout out: "Indeed, we have been overlooked. None has ever broken to us the bread of life or passed unto us the cup."

Where Suffering And Glory Blend

"If so be that we suffer with him, that we
may be also glorified together."
(Romans 8:17)

_____

THIS VERSE TAKES US to the position where suffering and glory blend. Suffering is a thing we avoid. Everyone flees from it. Who needs to suffer? We hide out inspired by a paranoid fear of meeting the fear thing on life's street. We assemble obstructions and build fortresses, however suffering giggles at us.

It brambles aside all of our barriers. It runs us down. It springs from a trap. It is hard of hearing to our cries and oblivious in regards to our miserable situation. We can't avoid suffering. Some it smites with physical torment, some with an anguished personality, some with debilitation and misery, some with the distress of a broken heart. Some place, once in a while on every life suffering during makes its imprint.

Glory is the thing we look for. Everyone is pursuing it. Everyone needs glory or something to that affect. There are numerous kinds of glory,- the glory of place, of power, of culture, of character, of expertise, of valor, of sacrifice, of affection, of unselfishness. There is the glory of the fighter, the statesman, the donor, the writer, the craftsman, the performer. Glory has numerous clothes, but whatever its piece of clothing, it is the thing everyone is after. Be that as it may, it is slippery. It hangs out. It disappears and abandons us in the unhappiness.

Suffering and Glory! The one thing all look for and the one thing all evade! We find them far separated, but this line from Paul's letter to the Romans appears to said: "If you will listen to me, I will show how suffering and glory blend and become one.

If you will harken to my voice and receive what I offer, you will discover suffering transfigured and glory acquired. "For if so be that we suffer with him, we shall also be glorified with him."

Glory Costs Suffering

WE GET A LOOK at this as we look about us in the world. It shows itself in nature. There was never a harvest but needed to pay the cost of torment and travail, never a first light but needed to drag itself out of the darkness of night, never a triumph but had the muck of slaughter on its trail, never a deed of bravery but someone needed to suffer. Glory is not modest, it is not cheap.

It's anything but a kind of ripe fruit which lazy hands may pluck from low hanging branches parts of an idle day. Glory camps on the heights. It is a cliff dweller. It costs, and the kind of coin in which installment must be made is stamped with suffering.

There is a place where we get more than a glimpse of the fact that glory cost suffering,- where we get a showing. There is a place where this great truth is proclaimed. It is at the cross. "If so be that we suffer with him, that we may be also glorified together." Calvary is the story of affliction, of suffering. Jesus was the great sufferer. Never was there agony like His. He drank the unpleasant cup (the bitter cup) to its residue. He abided in the anguish, in gloom which drifts about the natural hollows of death.

His heart anguished with a loneliness which appeared to isolate Him from God, but in this He was paying the price for the glory of becoming the world's Redeemer. He suffered all together that He may save. Had He never suffered, He could never save. This is the price He paid. At Calvary glory cost suffering.

Suffering Produces Glory

WE GET A SUGGESTION, a glimpse of this, as well, as we look out on the world about us. Nature likewise uncovers it in the ice which pummels the dirt for the new sowing, in the lightning which improves and sanitizes the air, in the dissenting nerves which ring the risk motions in our flesh against moving toward danger, in those suffering mind-sets of the soul by which human nature is enhanced with a gentler and a more extensive sympathy.

Suffering produces glory. You can see it in the refiner's pot where dross is devoured and gold is refined. You can see it on the potter's wheel where dull dirt is formed into use and beauty. You can see it under the hand of the lapidarian as the light shimmers and flashes from the face of a pearl, and you can see it in the great loom of time which weaves a texture we call life. Suffering produces glory. Glory is the completed result of suffering.

In any case, there is where we get more of an impression or a glimpse, where we get a demonstration. There is where it is proclaimed. It is at the cross, the cross of Calvary. The cross is the narrative of Jesus Christ's triumph. It lets us know not merely that He suffered. It was the place He achieved His dream.

As He hung there in the darkness, He saw the light. He saw past the thin layouts of the abhorrent tree (the cross), past His persecuters, past the nails and thorns and depression.

He saw past the veil into the glory. He saw the crown of conquest and the throne of dominion and the faces of companions, and He heard the triumph song. "He saw of the travail of his soul and was satisfied."

Thus this again is the place suffering and glory blend,- there where a Man laid down His life for a cause, and where along a street that was steep and harsh He move to the sun kissed tops, and where on a cross that was forlorn He hung until the night was gone, and where in a tomb that was sealed and guarded He nursed His expectation till Easter morning rolled the stone away and the angels said: "He is risen."

The Message Of The Ordinance
(The Lord's Supper)

THE HOLY ORDINANCE OR the Lord's Supper speaks to us of suffering,- not simply of our sufferings, but of the Savior's sufferings. It lets us know of One Who bore on His extraordinary heart every one of the sufferings of the world, Who carried on His shoulder every one of the burdens of humanity, and Who as He took His lot tasted death for every man.

It also speaks to us of glory,- not of a glory that is fake, not of the glory of place and grandeur and power, not of the glimmer of mortal triumph, but of eternal glory, of the glory which Jesus Christ had with the Father before the world was. It tells us of a spiritual glory that can never be dulled nor dimmed nor diminished.

Dr. John Thomas Wylie

And after that it reveals to us where these two things blend. It reveals to us that glory cost suffering and that suffering produces glory, and it pronounces that for the individuals who are with Him the chasm between glory and suffering vanishes. There is no promise or hope just to naked suffering. It is to the individuals who suffer with Him. Our sufferings must be with Jesus Christ. We should be His confidants, His friends.

It is the point at which we are in fellowship with Him that suffering is transfigured, and such fellowship is inside our scope (our reach), for Jesus says: "Let us suffer together that we may be also glorified together." This is the thing that He implies when He says: "Take my yoke upon you." He would lead us out where the thing we disregard turns into the thing we look for, and where our fears are changed to hope.

Let us not fear suffering, for if we suffer with Him we will also be glorified together. Whenever agony and anguish and distress break on us, let us consider Him Who remains close to us in the shadows and suffers, as well.

Let us remember that it pleased God to make the Captain of our salvation flawless, perfect through suffering, and realize that suffering can have no other mission for those in fellowship with Jesus Christ.

It is to make us immaculate. When we suffer, it is that our service might be bigger, better, holier. "I have called thee to suffer," was Jesus Christ's message to Paul. It was anything but a call to an overshadowed and reducing, but to an augmented and regularly expanding service. In this manner let us sit tight through the first part of the day. For the morning cometh. Trust that the haze of suffering will change to gold.

You have seen clouds do that there over the western slopes at dusk. You have viewed the morose sky sheathed in dark and agony change and fire into brilliant glory. It is an image of what goes to the individuals who suffer with Him. "For I reckon that the sufferings of this present time are not worthy to be compared with the glory that will be revealed in us." "For these light afflictions which are but for a moment will work out for us a far more exceeding and eternal weight of glory."

Thus for all who tarry at the cross and sit at the table, for all who drink of His cup and break the bread and are baptized through water with His baptism, suffering and glory blend.

Dr. John Thomas Wylie

From The Communion Table To Prejury

"If I should die with thee, I will not deny thee
in any wise. Likewise said they all."
(Mark 14:31)

THIS IS AN EXTRAORDINARY pledge of fealty to Jesus Christ. It is a relentless promise of faithfulness, a brilliant presentation of resolute faith and unfaltering commitment.

Jesus appears to be miserable. He is nearly on the verge of Calvary. He is entering upon a night of desolation. He is going through the entryway into Gethsemane. Addressing His followers about the dejection that will before long arrive, He discloses to them that they will abandon Him. They will destroy the shepherd and the sheep will be dispersed. There is a tinge of despairing sadness to His words as He predicts the abandonment of His followers.

It was then that Simon Peter made an extraordinary vow, and swore undying connection to Christ. "In the event that I should die with thee, I won't deny thee in any wise." Peter was never more noteworthy than at that point. He was on the summit of chivalrous love. If no one but he could live there dependably and be as valid, as undaunted, and straightforward in his devotion, what a power he would be!

He would not joke about this. Don't for a minute think he was imagining. What he said is more than unimportant words. Peter had his deficiencies, (his faults) however fraud was not one of them. He implied all that he said. His heart was fixed, and he was prepared without further ado to die for Jesus Christ.

In any case, he broke his vow, and lied himself. It was done under the most embarrassing conditions. Taken a look in the later happenings of that terrible night, what he said was more terrible than a brag or boast. It turned into the broken pledge (vow) of a liar, and stands halfway between the hour of holiest benefit and despicable disavowal (his shameful denial)

The Story

JESUS CHRIST HAD RECENTLY instituted the Lord's Supper. There in the upper room He was gathered with His disciples on the decisive night. It was the latest hour of serene, solid fellowship before the tempest. In His magnificent talk he had uncovered to them His heart. He had offered the intercessory prayer. How close they appeared to one another at that point, and how near God! At that point came the bread and the cup of remembrance, and afterward, the song, and now they are en route to the Mount of Olives.

It was the first communion ever in the history of the Church, the first festivity of the feast that should have been kept again and again. These men have shared it, have viewed the very essence of Christ, have heard His voice in the law, have seen Him touch and bless the emblems. Definitely they can never go from a scene so heavenly but to a service sacred and divine. No wonder they swear loyalty and state they are prepared to die for Him!

However in a couple of hours all is changed. Jesus Christ has been captured and His disciples, neglecting Him, have fled. The men who swore they would die with Him break their vow and keep running for their lives. There in the council chamber of the high priest Jesus Christ is on trial, the very

Christ Who at the communion table some time prior stated: "This do in remembrance of me."

Among those who steal into the servants' corridor on one side of the court is Peter. His cloak is gravitated toward about him. He is turbaned in order to be barely conspicuous. The night air is nippy and he gravitates toward the flame to warm himself.

Then the most low preliminary that at any point disrespected the chronicles of a court goes on. Jesus is summoned. The Savior is presently among His adversaries. They accuse Him of sacrilege, blasphemy. They take chamber to slaughter Him. They spit in His face and smite Him with the palms of their hands and pile coarse scorn on the gentle Christ. How does the supporter take this? How does the man who stated: "If I should die with thee I will not deny thee in any wise," handle himself now?

He warms himself. He is making himself comfortable. Straightforwardly a maid says: "And thou also wast with Jesus of Nazareth!" But he denied, saying: "I know not, neither understand I what thou sayest." This is the man who five hours before had sat at the communion table and said: "I will remember."

Also, straightforwardly a servant saw him once more, and started to state to them that stood by: "This is one of them," and again he denied. This is the man who three hours before had pronounced he would die sooner than deny. He has perjured himself. At that point one who stood by stated: "Surely thou art one of them, for thou art a Galilean, and thy speech agreeth thereto."

In any case, he started to revile and to swear, saying: "I know not this man of whom ye speak." And yet his lips are hardly dry from the communion wine, and the breath of his vow is still all over his face. In six brief hours Simon Peter has dove from the heights to the depths.

How might he do a thing such as this? He has pursued Jesus for a long time and seen Him work miracles. He has walked on the sea to meet Him and been available at the transfiguration. He has pronounced: "Thou art the Christ, the Son of the Living God!" How under any conditions would he be able to get his consent to deny his Master? How might he do it the situation being what it is of the preliminary and with the torment, abandoned Savior only there through the entryway? It was the ideal opportunity for him to surge in, and stand by and die, but rather, with pledges and reviles he denies his Master.

Furthermore, the Bible records this account of disgrace. We don't get it from Christ's foes, however from His friends. The Bible has nothing to disguise. In the event that it were a human book such an episode would be forgotten, erased or disregarded. In any case, the Book is divine. It tells all. It records the vow, and after that relates how the central witness go from that incredible vow to perjury.

What does this prove? Not that Christianity is false, nor Jesus Christ a faker, nor His lessons without esteem, nor the hour in the upper room unimportant. It doesn't mark Christian faith as a misleading thing, and brand Christ's disciples as wolves in sheep's clothing. It just demonstrates that men may fizzle, that the best of men may fall into the most noticeably bad of sins, that human nature is frail, that allurement is incessant, and that men of the most elevated blessings and the most extravagant experience once in a while drop from statures of faith to depths of apostasy.

Application

PRIVILEGE DOES NOT PREVENT sin. The way that one appreciates uncommon spiritual blessings does not safeguard against the likelihood of a fall. One might be blessed with every one of the means for grace. He may originate from a Christian home where the Bible and the prayer life obtain. He might be an individual from the church and receive the ordinance.

He might be regenerated and have a precious spiritual ordeal and appreciate times of incredible spiritual elation, but then go down in some great moral or spiritual breakdown.

The fact that one is a Christian, that he has experienced regeneration and become an offspring of God and a beneficiary to glory, does not promise him against the likelihood of falling into wrongdoing (sin). Once in a while we assume it does, and envision that when one has become a christian the battle is finished. Be that as it may, not really. Frequently the genuine battle has recently started. Temptation is even more deceptive and troublesome after one has stood firm and started to stay the course of faith.

The Scriptures over and over record cases of the fall of God's servants. David was a man after God's own heart, however he fell. There is certifiably not an perfect man in the Old Testament. Peter was not the only one. Every one of the disciples fled. Today is the equivalent. Great men turn out badly. Here and there some preachers of the Gospel are blameworthy of the notoriety which wrecks a home. They direct the ordinance and afterward go on to deeds in which they deny their Lord.

It is a blessed, holy privilege to come to communion, to gather with Christ's friends around the table and partake of the ordinance (the Lord's Supper, Communion), to remember Jesus and plight to Him once again our troth, to state in act if not in words: "In the event that I should die with thee, I won't deny thee in any wise." Let us not, nonetheless, infer that there is no risk of a fall for us.

It is conceivable to go from the table to drunkenness, to infidelity, to deceitfulness. The lips which touch the emblems of communion may profane1 God's name and deny the Savior. The man who sat at the table may straightforwardly be sitting with Christ's foes. "Let him that thinketh he standeth take heed lest he fall." Privilege does not prevent sin.

There is no wall against temptation, no obstruction that can keep it out, no defensive layer that makes us safe. It found Jesus Christ., Jesus was enticed, and His temptation came not long after His Baptism, not long after the voice from paradise affirming His Sonship with God.

No preacher's home, no devout house, no blessed retreat, no hallowed calling, can make us exempt. Some of the time the hazard of temptation appears to be most prominent along the fringe of our holiest encounters. Satan comes to us in the wake of spiritual triumph and accomplishment. He surprises us. He takes in secret while we are flat footed, in some snapshot of great religious joy. In any case, don't reason that it is difficult to resist him. We don't have to yield to temptation.

It is the devil's lie to trust that since we are enticed we should fall, or that the nearness of temptation is a reason for surrender. Jesus Christ wouldn't yield. Temptation must be stood up to. When we resist the fallen angel (the devil) he flees from us. We can't escape temptation. It came to the angels, and it comes to men even in holiest minutes and places, but it tends to be fought off and vanquished.

Our fall does not ruin Christ. It is terrible on any cause when its followers turn out badly. People are disposed to blame

Dr. John Thomas Wylie

a cause for the weaknesses of its advocates. Jesus Christ's cause does not get away. At the point when Christians carry on severely and drag their robes in the dirt and degrade the high calling, the world is disposed to state: "Christ is a faker. The Gospel is a superstition. The Bible is false."

Privilege does not prevent sin. The way that one appreciates uncommon spiritual blessings does not safeguard against the likelihood of a fall. One might be blessed with every one of the means for grace. He may originate from a Christian home where the Bible and the prayer life obtain. He might be an individual from the church and receive the ordinance.

He might be regenerated and have a precious spiritual ordeal and appreciate times of incredible spiritual elation, but then go down in some great moral or spiritual breakdown.

The fact that one is a Christian, that he has experienced regeneration and become an offspring of God and a beneficiary to glory, does not promise him against the likelihood of falling into wrongdoing (sin). Once in a while we assume it does, and envision that when one has become a christian the battle is finished. Be that as it may, not really. Frequently the genuine battle has recently started. Temptation is even more deceptive and troublesome after one has stood firm and started to stay the course of faith.

The Scriptures over and over record cases of the fall of God's servants. David was a man after God's own heart, however he fell. There is certifiably not a perfect man in the Old Testament. Peter was not the only one. Every one of the disciples fled. Today is the equivalent. Great men turn out badly.

Here and there some preachers of the Gospel are blameworthy of the notoriety which wrecks a home. They direct the ordinance and afterward go on to deeds in which they deny their Lord.

It is a blessed, holy privilege to come to communion, to gather with Christ's friends around the table and partake of the ordinance (the Lord's Supper, Communion), to remember Jesus and plight to Him once again our troth, to state in act if not in words: "In the event that I should die with thee, I won't deny thee in any wise." Let us not, nonetheless, infer that there is no risk of a fall for us.

It is conceivable to go from the table to drunkenness, to infidelity, to deceitfulness. The lips which touch the emblems of communion may profane1 God's name and deny the Savior. The man who sat at the table may straightforwardly be sitting with Christ's foes. "Let him that thinketh he standeth take heed lest he fall." Privilege does not prevent sin.

There is no wall against temptation, no obstruction that can keep it out, no defensive layer that makes us safe. It found Jesus Christ., Jesus was enticed, and His temptation came not long after His Baptism, not long after the voice from paradise affirming His Sonship with God. No preacher's home, no devout house, no blessed retreat, no hallowed calling, can make us exempt.

Some of the time the hazard of temptation appears to be most prominent along the fringe of our holiest encounters. Satan comes to us in the wake of spiritual triumph and accomplishment. He surprises us. He takes in secret while we are flat footed, in some snapshot of great religious joy. In any case, don't reason that it is difficult to resist him. We don't have to yield to temptation.

It is the devil's lie to trust that since we are enticed we should fall, or that the nearness of temptation is a reason for surrender. Jesus Christ wouldn't yield. Temptation must be stood up to. When we resist the fallen angel (the devil) he flees from us. We can't escape temptation. It came to the angels, and it comes to men even in holiest minutes and places, but it tends to be fought off and vanquished.

Our fall does not ruin Christ. It is terrible on any cause when its followers turn out badly. People are disposed to blame a cause for the weaknesses of its advocates. Jesus Christ's cause does not get away. At the point when Christians carry on severely and drag their robes in the dirt and degrade the high calling, the world is disposed to state: "Christ is a faker. The Gospel is a superstition. The Bible is false."

Can The World
Reproduce Calvary?

"We ought to lay down our lives for the brethren."
(I John 3:16)

THIS IS A BOLD thing for a man to said. Does he understand what his words mean? It is safe to say that he is beating the air or would he say he is prepared for business? We should lay down lives for the brethren. This implies the people who speak to Jesus Christ on earth should meet Him at Calvary.

They should meet Him there not to sing psalms and discuss rituals, not to take cover behind the skirts of a catastrophe that is to make them safe from punishment, not to exploit a doctrine or buying in to authoritative opinions which establish their sign of universality.

They are to meet Him there at Calvary to die with Him, to match His passion with sacrifice, to become companions of the cross and lay down their lives for the brethren.

Thus the world is to be saved. Jesus did not die just to satisfy us or to make us happy. It is a modest determination that discovers nothing more gallant, more heroic in Calvary than exemption. Those who think about the Gospel as a plan to play "security first," as a task to rebuild the lost Eden, as an after death visa to Heaven, have not walked the thorn path with the Son of God.

Jesus Christ died for us that we may die for other people, in light of the fact that the only street to life for anything twists past a grave, on the grounds that the only hope in this or any world is in people who love enough to make the supreme sacrifice..

The communion would keep this in everlasting remembrance. Jesus Christ's death is saying that we ought lay down our lives for the brethren. It is a striking thing to said that we will. Is it excessively strong? Is it so brave that none can be found to meet it? Is it vain to hope that in the earth today may be found some with hearts prepared and souls aflame to venture out of the ranks and say: "We are ready"?

Peter said: "I will die for Him." True, he flopped, however he had one wonderful moment when his soul was sufficiently enormous enough to state it and to mean it. Some who are prepared to state to such an extent and make good the vow must be found today, else civilization is doomed and the world lost.

The World Outlook

THESE ARE DAYS WHEN the world is brimming with struggle, terrorism, and turmoil. Powers have been discharged which compromise to devastate the sum total of what that has been picked up by the work and battle of humankind. Perspectives on human relations are being advanced which, whenever set in motion, would make hellfire a delight resort in correlation with earth.

Governments are disintegrating, crumbling. Nothing any more appears to be sacred and holy. It has been recommended that even God Himself be canceled. Within the sight of this mob of irreverence and political agitation, the faith of some wavers and comes up short. The standpoint is dull and foreboding. Men are asking: "Is civilization an inconceivable dream?"

There is, nonetheless, another side to the circumstance. There are components in the outlook which imply a human proficiency and accomplishment never outperformed. Man is all the more totally possessing the dominance of material powers than at any other time. His disclosures have wrested from nature a portion of its profoundest mysteries.

His creations have tackled land, ocean, and sky, and made them his servants to a degree before undreamed. He has endeavored the outlandish and in certain occurrences has achieved it. What is there that he can't do? He has domain over each domain. He can manage anything. Truly, anything other than himself.

One does not need to be insightful to discover there is little hope for restoring world agitation through man's dominance of nature and science, of exchange and innovation. Man was never to a greater extent a superman than he is today, and the insufficiency of his dominance of world powers to set up a rational social request was never progressively evident.

Something more is needed to fix this slanted, crooked world, to disgrace its desire and kill its childishness, to demolish sacrilege and set up righteousness, honesty, to vanquish abhor and encourage cooperative attitude, something more is expected to harness the permit which runs wild on the planet today, and convey us from hazards which compromise to make human progress unimaginable, something more by a long shot is required than a superman's domain over nature. What's going on here?

We shall not find its short of Calvary. We are powerless until we fall back on the cross. What the world needs today isn't enthusiasm to collect but willingness to spend, not virtuoso for acing material powers but rather a dream of spiritual values, not desire for power but rather passion for service, not a roost in the sun but rather a cross on a hillcrest. The world needs a fresh infusion of the sacrificial spirit.

We need the eyes of Calvary to consider men to be as Jesus Christ saw them from the cross. They were not adversaries He saw, however they drove the nails through His hands, for He supplicated: "Father, forgive them." They were not hoodlums, or enemies for He said to the criminal: "Today thou shalt be with me in Paradise." They were His brothers. When we can look into a man's face, regardless of whether he be worker or entrepreneur, whether he be American, British or African or of some other ethnic foundation or country, and see what the cross crowned Jesus Christ saw, the broken world will start to heal.

We need the heart of Calvary, to feel toward men as Jesus Christ felt as He hung there on the cross. Jesus did not despise them nor dread them. He loved them, since He died for them. He was more on edge to help them than to deliver Himself. He could have descended from the cross and declined sacrifice. It was love that kept Him there. It is love this well worn world needs, not virtuoso, not cerebrums, not statesmanship, not cash and power, simply love; and God is love.

We need the passion of the cross. We need the passion of Calvary. Then we shall accomplish for men what Jesus Christ did. He was no profiteer, no wanton striker. He died for us. Neither man nor God could go further. "Greater love hath no man than this." What society needs isn't to slaughter off a great deal of nuisances or undesirables. To make certain violence and savagery must be punished and political agitation stamped out, but the world will never be cleared of upset by slaughtering individuals.

There must be some who choose to die for the brethren if the world is ever to have a better day. This is the challenge the world tosses at the Church. Would we be able to reproduce Calvary? Would we be able to reenact the cross?

The Challenge

IT IS A CHALLENGE Christian men can't overlook. The Church has gone to its greatest open door since Calvary. The estimation of what it brings to the table was never increasingly obvious. Men are seeing that the destinations of the Christian Church are those of any human civilization worth having. As at no other time, the sick world is swinging to the Church for some assistance. The Church is up close and personal with its biggest chance, its most compelling hour, since Calvary.

There are confirmations (evidences) that the Church is waking to the challenge and endeavoring to shape its lines for bigger things than man has ever yet endeavored in God's name. A portion of these plans are so immense, so broad, so crushing of point of reference, so progressive as to stun and dumbfound. Regardless of whether they are the crotchets of insane lovers or the statesmanship of a Caleb-like faith for the future to uncover.

Be that as it may, any development that is to address the issues of the present reality must accomplish more than immaculate a mind blowing association and undertaking its plans on a world scale. It must do that. It must utilize apparatus and attention and official capacity and everything that is a benefit anywhere for God and His kingdom. Be that as it may, this must be soaked totally with the spirit of Calvary. The men who are behind the organization must be men who are friends of the cross.

Will this century (2019) and beyond reproduce Calvary? It can fund-raise. It can hold enormous traditions. It can gather numbers and arouse enthusiasm, however can it lay down its life? Would it be able to create people who intentionally, choose to remain poor, who are content with obscurity, who are willing sit tight for results, and if needs be, die with the nails in their hands and the thorns on their forehead?

For such people the world waits. There is an incentive in sacrifice which earth can't measure. It is sacrifice that brings us up close and personal with the only power that can save the world. It is sacrifice that lifts mediocrity to genius and widens provincialism out into world citizenship.

The Sacrificial Spirit

WHAT THE WORLD NEEDS today is a bigger proportion of the sacrificial spirit, not of the sacrifice that is staggering or that is punitive, but of the sacrifice that serves. It was a dead world to which Jesus Christ came two thousand years prior. It had consumed itself out in transgression (sin).

Its standards had spoiled down in extravagance and liberality. Egotism, criticism, uncertainty, and sadness were on each hand. Into that universe of disgrace and rot, of sexiness and decrepit depression, Christ built Calvary, and from the hour He died on the cross there was hope.

Would Calvary be able to be incorporated with the cutting edge world? In 2019? It is no not as much as this that Jesus expects of His adherents. He isn't requesting influence and riches and organization. He is requesting sacrifice, for individuals who are so entirely committed to Him and the cause for which He died that they are prepared to die, as well.

I don't imply that any man can atone for wrongdoing (sin), that our cross can ever be a substitute for His cross, but in the event that His cross is genuine to me, it must be an experience, and not just a memory.

It is safe to say that we are prepared for the cross? Is it true that we are prepared to carry it, to hold tight to it, to get crucified? What are we out for? The greatest issue before the world isn't internationalism or labor unionism or any other "isms". It isn't the red peril. It is the red hope, the scarlet, blood dyed hope of Calvary!

Memory And Hope At The Communion Table

"This do in remembrance of me." "Christ Jesus our hope."
(Luke 22:19; I Tim. 1:1)

As GATHERED AT THE communion table, it is to keep the Lord's Supper, Jesus Christ's friends keep the feast of love, to celebrate the ordinance by which faith pledges anew its loyalty to the Saviour..

Memory

IT IS AN HOUR for memory. Jesus Christ founded the Lord's Supper to shield His people from overlooking Him. "This do in remembrance of me." As we approach the communion table, let memory cast its spell.

Let us remember what that old world was when Jesus was crucified. It was a wild world. Power was in charge. An expansive piece of mankind was in subjugation. Numbness, ignorance, and superstition were across the board. Viciousness, Violence and wrongdoing were the order of the day. Corruption so base that it must be recommended instead of examined was common.

Urban communities were cesspools of injustice, and government a name for mistreatment and oppression. This was the sort of world in which Jesus Christ lived. Let us not forget those days. Remembering them, we will be less enticed to lose hope in these.

For it is something of a wild world still. Powers which compromise and threaten society have broken their rope, and except if rebuked and limited or restrained will result in across the board fiasco (widespread disaster). There is as still the scourge of numbness, lack of education, superstition, still the unpleasant hand of brutality, the red eye of desire, and the trickling claw of greed. Be that as it may, the world is less wild than it was.

If Jesus Christ did not lose hope, at that point, we need not today. If He saw enough of good in that wild world of ancient times to die for it, without a doubt we can discover enough of good in our own to live for it. This is no time for misery. Give us a chance to remember until faith develops suffering and we take a crisp hold on our work.

Let us remember that blamelessness suffered (innocence suffered). Jesus Christ did not deserve the treatment He got. He was no criminal. His was the gentlest and the purest life the world has known. His was the gentlest spirit that ever breathed among us.

Jesus was the best man Who walked the earth. But He suffered, and His sufferings were genuine and great. Men suffer as indicated by their power to feel as opposed to as per the blow that is struck. Jesus Christ's power to feel was vast. His sufferings were indefinable. What's more, withal, He was blameless, innocent.

When we suffer without cause, let us remember Jesus Christ. It is difficult to suffer when one is aware of his innocence. If anything can make a man abhor society, it is for society to punish him for a wrongdoing of which he isn't blameworthy. If there is anything that makes it hard to love high beliefs and continue attempting to do right, it is to realize that you have not had a square deal.

In any case, when we are tempted to throw down our apparatuses and quit in light of the fact that those we have endeavored to help neglected to play reasonable, let memory lead us by the hand into the presence of that white light that was driven as a sheep to the butcher (slaughter).

Let us remember that Calvary was not an annihilation nor defeat. It looked as though hate had triumphed. As Jesus Christ hung there on the cross and His foes throw dice for His seamless robe, and Herod and Caiaphas praised themselves on the effective achievement of the dirtiest day's work of history records, it looked as though virtue was whipped. Be that as it may, we know since it was not, that Calvary was Christ's supreme victory, that from that cross He had His crown.

We must remember that the cross is always this, and when we go to our Calvary, let us not be absolutely thrown down. Again and again the soul that attempts to save the world must submit to torturous killing, the crucifixion, but as the nails are driven in and the thorns and the lance, let each one who cherishes a cause superior to anything he does his life remember the green hill far away, and Jesus Who hung there until He became so lonely that He thought even God had forsaken Him. Remembering this, unhappiness and sadness will vanish.

Let us remember that Jesus Christ loved us. I could agree to surrender everything except for this, and still feel that I had enough left to make the morning beyond any doubt. In any case, in the event that I will ever reach an hour when I feel that Jesus Christ's love is dead, I will realize that the night has vanquished, and that I am lost.

Jesus Christ died on the cross to prove His love, a love so high that the highest sky are not higher, so profound that the base of hellfire isn't more profound, so steady that time can't transform it, so consistent that time everlasting can't destroy it.

Gracious, to be capable with all holy people to fathom the love that passeth knowledge! At the holy communion table let us remember the Savior's love.

If we will, we can stand anything. There is much we can't see, but if Jesus Christ loves us, we know that God is our Friend. If He is, the trap of destiny (the web of fate) will unravel, and the long, winding road will end where welcome holds on to welcome the weary.

Hope

Thus the Lord's Supper (Holy Communion) is a place for memory, but for hope. Jesus Christ is our hope. As we look out on the wild present world, let us trust since we believe in Jesus Christ. He can deal with the circumstances of a wild world. With such a gospel, I am happy to be a preacher, since I have the solution for a sin sick world, the main appeal that will tame its ferocity, the main call that will draw it from its wilderness and change it from a dread to a companion.

When we are wronged, consider Jesus Christ, and remain sweet, and stay unfaltering. Bad form isn't perpetual. Life's extraordinary reward isn't what men may think. It is to hear His dear lips state: "Well done."

When the battle looks lost, let us think about the crucified Christ, and battle on. We must think about the annihilations that have been changed to triumphs. We tumble to rise. "These light afflictions which are but a moment shall work out for us a far more exceeding and eternal weight of glory."

Furthermore, when the day is dark and the way is long, and the weight heavier than we can bear, let us think about

His love, until hope yet again begins its reasonable tune on our tired lips.

"This do in remembrance of me." "Jesus Christ our hope." Memory and hope at the communion table! These are the twin angels of the existence tranquil, and they welcome us at the table of the King of love. As we take the bread, let us remember.

As we touch to our lips the cup of His blood, let us hope. There is no death for the individuals who remember, and there is deathless victory for those who hope!

Bibliography

The Holy Bible (1964) Authorized King James Version. Chicago, Ill.: J. G. Ferguson

The Holy Bible (1982) New International Version. Grand Rapids, MI.: Thomas Nelson Inc. (Used By Permission)

The Holy Bible (1953) The Revised Standard Version. Nashville, TN.: Thomas Nelson And Sons (Used By Permission)

The Holy Bible (1901) The American Standard Version. Nashville, TN.: Thomas Nelson (Used By Permission)

The Holy Bible (2017) The New International Version. Grand Rapids, MI.: Zondervan Corporation (Used By Permission)

The Wycliff Bible Commentary (1962) Nashville, TN.: The Southwestern Company,

The Moody Bible Institute Of Chicago

About The Author

THE REVEREND DR. JOHN **Thomas Wylie** is one who has dedicated his life to the work of God's Service, the service of others; and being a powerful witness for the Gospel of Our Lord and Savior Jesus Christ. Dr. Wylie was called into the Gospel Ministry June 1979, whereby in that same year he entered The American Baptist College of the American Baptist Theological Seminary, Nashville, Tennessee.

As a young Seminarian, he read every book available to him that would help him better his understanding of God as well as God's plan of Salvation and the Christian Faith. He made a commitment as a promising student that he would inspire others as God inspires him. He understood early in his ministry that we live in times where people question not only who God is; but whether miracles are real, whether or not man can make a change, and who the enemy is or if the enemy truly exists.

Dr. Wylie carried out his commitment to God, which has been one of excellence which led to his earning his Bachelors of Arts in Bible/Theology/Pastoral Studies. Faithful and obedient to the call of God, he continued to matriculate in his studies earning his Masters of Ministry from Emmanuel Bible College, Nashville, Tennessee & Emmanuel Bible College, Rossville, Georgia. Still, inspired to please the Lord and do that which is well – pleasing in the Lord's sight, Dr. Wylie recently on March 2006, completed his Masters of Education degree with a concentration in Instructional Technology earned at The American Intercontinental University, Holloman Estates, Illinois. Dr. Wylie also previous to this, earned his Education

Specialist Degree from Jones International University, Centennial, Colorado and his Doctorate of Theology from The Holy Trinity College and Seminary, St. Petersburg, Florida.

Dr. Wylie has served in the capacity of pastor at two congregations in Middle Tennessee and Southern Tennessee, as well as served as an Evangelistic Preacher, Teacher, Chaplain, Christian Educator, and finally a published author, writer of many great inspirational Christian Publications such as his first publication: *"Only One God: Who Is He?" – published August 2002 via formally 1ˢᵗ books library (which is now AuthorHouse Book Publishers located in Bloomington, Indiana & Milton Keynes, United Kingdom)* which caught the attention of **The Atlanta Journal Constitution Newspaper.**

Dr. Wylie is happily married to Angel G. Wylie, a retired Dekalb Elementary School teacher who loves to work with the very young children and who always encourages her husband to move forward in the Name of Jesus Christ. They have Four children, 11 grand-children and one great-grandson all of whom they are very proud. Both Dr. Wylie and Angela Wylie serve as members of the Salem Baptist Church, located in Lilburn, Georgia, where the Reverend Dr. Richard B. Haynes is Senior pastor.

Dr. Wylie has stated of his wife: "she knows the charm and beauty of sincerity, goodness, and purity through Jesus Christ. Yes, she is a Christian and realizes the true meaning of loveliness as the reflection as her life of holy living gives new meaning, hope, and purpose to that of her husband, her children, others may say of her, "Behold the handmaiden of the Lord." A Servant of Jesus Christ!

About The Book

THIS PUBLICATION, "THE BREAKING Of The Bread," contains messages on The Lord's Supper (Holy Communion) which resembles the "Holy of holies" in Christian experience. Better for every one of us if our love for that high hour at the communion table were more noteworthy. Better for the Church if the blessed fellowship of the Presence could cast its spell on present day life until love feels its praising touch.

The Christian has discovered a place whose spirit is elevated and gathered by the very idea of the communion, until one purposes that nothing will be allowed to break his trust with his Savior.

It is with hope that these communion messages may develop such a mind-set, that I am sending them out. If they will coordinate reflection as the heart gets ready for the hour when we meet at the Lord's table; they will serve to enliven faith and arouse love; if they can by one way or another show his companions in any supportive way what "more noteworthy love" has done that He ought to be remembered, at that point these communion messages will fill their need.

"And the disciples devoted themselves to...breaking of the bread..." (Acts 2:42). "On the first day of the week, when we gathered to break bread..." (20:7). It holds a central place in our Christian worship.

Reverend Dr. John Thomas Wylie

Printed in the United States
By Bookmasters